IRONBRIDGE
HISTORY & GUIDE

IRONBRIDGE
HISTORY & GUIDE

Richard Hayman & Wendy Horton

The History Press

First published in 1999 by Tempus Publishing
Reprinted 2003, 2005

Reprinted in 2009 by
The History Press
The Mill, Brimscombe Port
Stroud, Gloucestershire GL5 2QG

Reprinted 2010, 2012

British Library Cataloguing in Publication Data.
A catalogue record for this book is available from the British Library.

ISBN 978 0 7524 1460 7

Typesetting and origination by Tempus Publishing.
Printed in Great Britain.

CONTENTS

ILLUSTRATIONS

The authors are grateful to their colleagues at the Ironbridge Gorge Museum for help in rounding up the illustrations, especially to John Powell, Katie Foster, Kate Cadman and Melanie Heywood. We are grateful to Lord Forester for granting access to the Forester records at the Shropshire Records and Research Centre and for allowing the plan of Caughley Chinaworks to be reproduced here.

The copyright holders of the photographs are: Lord Forester (35); Richard Hayman (3, 4, 13, 51, 52, 53, 54, 56, 57, 58, 59, 62, 65, 66, 67, 69, 70, 71, 73, 74, 75; colour plates 18, 19, 20, 22, 24, 25); Ironbridge Gorge Museum Trust (1, 7, 8, 9, 10, 11, 12, 15, 16, 17, 18, 19, 20, 21, 22, 25, 26, 27, 28, 29, 30, 31, 32, 33, 34, 36, 37, 38, 39, 40, 41, 42, 43, 44, 45, 46, 48, 50, 55, 60, 61, 63, 64, 68, 72; colour plates 1, 2, 3, 4, 6, 7, 8, 9, 10, 11, 12, 13, 14, 15, 16, 17, 23); Science Museum (23, 24); Shropshire Records and Research Centre (2, 5, 6, 14, 47); Shropshire Archaeological and Historical Society (49); Shrewsbury Museums Service (colour plate 5); Skyscan Balloon Photography (colour plate 21).

Black & white Figures

Colour Plates

The cover illustration shows the Iron Bridge by William Williams, commissioned in 1780 by Abraham Darby III.

1
INTRODUCTION

The Iron Bridge across the River Severn is one of the landmarks of the industrial revolution (**1**). An audacious technical achievement spanning a notoriously volatile river, and an eloquent argument for the aesthetic possibilities of cast iron, the bridge was an international phenomenon even before it was completed, eulogised in the Houses of Parliament and marvelled at by European and American visitors. Built in 1779 and opened in 1781, the Iron Bridge was the perfect symbol of the Enlightenment, when technological innovation promised limitless possibilities for the improvement of life.

Its engineers, alas, gained little financial rewards for their efforts, a characteristic we have come to regard as typically British. But Abraham Darby III, who toiled heroically to see the bridge erected, was born into a culture of achievement. His grandfather Abraham Darby I stands with James Watt and Thomas Newcomen as one of the giants of British innovation. At the beginning of the eighteenth century he successfully substituted charcoal for coke in the smelting of iron, a breakthrough that was to see thousands of people leave home and migrate to the coalfields during the industrial revolution. Here also successive members of the Darby family and their Quaker compatriots pioneered the use of iron rails and steam engines. Meanwhile their rivals across the river in Broseley were inventing boats with iron hulls and efficient machines for boring the cannon with which the British fought Trafalgar and Waterloo.

The success stimulated by the iron and coal industries led to the development of other industries. This development was pioneered by men like William Reynolds, who had the energy and imagination to found a new town at Coalport, where the famous chinaworks was established, and who encouraged new developments in civil engineering and steam technology. At the end of the eighteenth century, the heyday of industry in Ironbridge, this obscure corner of England could claim to be the most technologically advanced district in the world, the Silicon Valley of its day. The iron industry declined in the nineteenth century, but its place was taken by the manufacture of pottery, bricks and decorative tiles. These new products were based upon the exploitation of local clays, and their development charts the story of applied arts in Victorian Britain. The cheap transport offered by the River Severn, to be superseded in the mid-nineteenth century by the railways, enabled local products to be exported across Britain and its Empire. Cast iron was used to build bridges, while domestic iron wares were distributed nation-wide or left Bristol to be traded for slaves in Africa; churchwarden tobacco pipes were fashionable in London coffee houses, Broseley roof tiles were a ubiquitous if not always welcome feature of nineteenth-century buildings, while the versatile decorative tiles of Maws and Craven Dunnill adorned shops, offices, public houses and homes.

1 *The Iron Bridge, painted by John Nash in 1950. Nash was one of a number of artists to take an interest in the industrial past in the early days of the conservation movement*

Although the term 'industrial revolution' is embedded in our vocabulary, historians and archaeologists no longer regard the concept as a single event with a beginning and an end. Rather, it is convenient shorthand for a process of cumulative change over a long period from the end of the middle ages, changes that accelerated so dramatically in the eighteenth and nineteenth centuries. The area around Ironbridge, often known as the Severn Gorge, was one of the first districts to experience these changes, and among the first to be left behind by them. The area symbolises and encapsulates much of the human condition over the last 300 years.

Historians have long been interested in the Darby family and the Coalbrookdale iron trade, and more recently archaeologists have turned their attention to the physical remains of the industrial revolution. The techniques applied by archaeologists to the post-medieval period are not always or solely the excavations with which they are traditionally associated. Close analysis of buildings, landscapes and artefacts, reference to historical sources such as Estate maps or Tithe maps, company accounts, legal papers, the views of artists, and sometimes oral history are all part of the eclectic approach to the archaeology of the industrial period (**2, colour plate 1**). The role of the archaeologist is to explain the buildings and landscapes of the period and help to ensure their preservation by recording them, seeing that they are sensitively restored and not blighted by unsuitable developments. To this extent archaeologists are curators of the historic environment in the

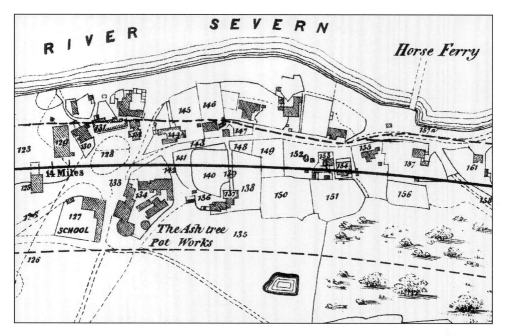

2 *Maps are a vital source of information for archaeologists studying the industrial revolution period. This map, surveyed to show the proposed Shropshire Union Railway in 1846, shows the Ash Tree Potworks, on the site of which the Craven Dunnill Tileworks was erected in 1871*

same sense that museum curators look after artefacts. As individuals and as a community, we all need places which are associated with our past and which tie us to the places we inhabit. Ironbridge fulfils a social need to understand our history and is a unique component in the make-up of British culture.

The pattern of the industrial revolution was one of boom when people migrated to new districts in search of employment, followed by depression as raw materials became exhausted, leaving a declining population and a shrunken economy. In this respect Ironbridge is typical, and was perhaps the first district in Britain to go through this cycle. Even during its best years the finite nature of industrial production based on the exploitation of raw materials was recognised. In 1754 Richard Ford of the Coalbrookdale Company told Charles Wood that 'both Coal & Ironstone will fail in 20 years, so that it will not be worth anyone's while to continue, or Erect other works there'.

In spite of its importance in the industrial revolution, Ironbridge suffered bleak years of decline and was hardly a picture postcard in the early twentieth century. A new spirit emerged in the mid century that spawned the now flourishing conservation movement, driven by the need to preserve aspects of a vulnerable historic environment at a time when there have been so many large-scale changes in our towns, cities and countryside. In the 1930s John Piper and John Betjeman delighted in the 'steps, terraces, bricks, weeds, more terraces' of Ironbridge and found in Broseley a 'decayed manufacturing town of great beauty'. Writing in 1958, the architectural historian Sir Nikolaus Pevsner thought the famous blast furnace at Coalbrookdale in a squalid state, made all the more regrettable as only a little money would be needed to give a little dignity to what was already regarded as an important monument to the industrial revolution.

In 1959 the Coalbrookdale Company, who had never ceased making cast iron at Coalbrookdale, tidied up and made a small museum around the surviving blast furnace to mark the 250th anniversary of Abraham Darby's adoption of coke smelting. It was during the 1960s, however, that conservation came to the fore. The Ironbridge Gorge Museum Trust was established in 1968 by the Telford Development Corporation and with a strong vein of volunteers. The new town of Telford was being constructed on derelict industrial land of the East Shropshire Coalfield, and its development from the 1970s has been paralleled by conservation in the Severn Gorge. Whereas at one time poor housing and idiosyncratic street layout would have been earmarked for demolition, in the Severn Gorge they were retained as part of the character of the district, and to maintain a sense of the past. As a result, Ironbridge found a new lease of life as a cultural commodity, heritage becoming the dominant player in the post-industrial economy. In recognition of the fact that so much of its historic character has been preserved, coupled with the influence that the area played in the nation's industrial development, the Ironbridge Gorge has been designated by UNESCO as a World Heritage Site.

Ironbridge is at the south end of the East Shropshire Coalfield, a relatively small coalfield less than 10 miles (16km) square. It is located on the River Severn between Shrewsbury and Bridgnorth, allowing its trade to be associated with those towns as well as the ports of Gloucester and Bristol. Its coal and iron trades were closely linked with the South Staffordshire Black Country, about 15 miles (24km) to the east, while its pottery trades were linked with the Potteries of North Staffordshire. Coal, ironstone, clay and limestone lay near the surface and could be worked with comparative ease at the south end of the coalfield. That is why industry developed there so early. Towards the north end of the coalfield the minerals lay at a greater depth and were consequently not exploited until the nineteenth century.

The Ironbridge or Severn Gorge defines the cluster of settlements on either side of the river (**3**). The gorge itself is a glacial feature, formed when the River Severn was diverted from its original course and cut through the south end of the coalfield, leaving its minerals conveniently exposed. The north side of the river was the manor of Madeley. The town stands well away from the river and spawned some detached industrial or riverside settlements such as Coalbrookdale, Ironbridge, Madeley Wood and Coalport. On the south side of the river are the ancient manors of Broseley and Benthall that spawned the riverside settlements of Jackfield and Bower Yard respectively. Further inland was the manor of Willey, these three districts marking the boundary of the coalfield, with Much Wenlock 3 miles (5km) to the west.

Life in Ironbridge has always been structured to a large extent by the River Severn. Even today flooding at the entrance to the Gorge is an almost annual event. Until the Iron Bridge was built the nearest bridges were at Buildwas and Bridgnorth, and ferries were the only means of crossing the river. Of the later bridges, the Iron Bridge has been closed to traffic since 1934 while traffic across the narrow Coalport Bridge is restricted, leaving the new Jackfield Bridge as the principal link between the two sides of the river.

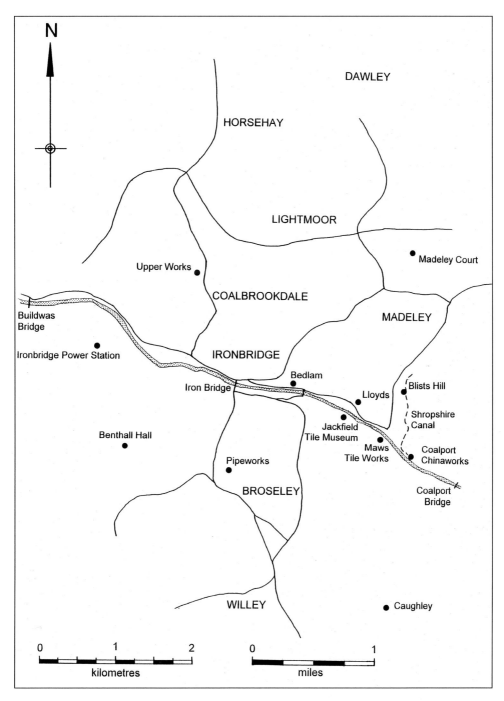

3 *The Ironbridge district, showing the main settlements and sites mentioned in the text*

The new town of Telford is to the north of Madeley and is composed of a number of small settlements, many of which, like Dawley, Ketley and Donnington Wood, are historically significant locations, although there are few remains of the industrial revolution to be seen there. Ironbridge is categorically the heritage zone of the former coalfield.

2
BEGINNINGS

In the early middle ages the landscape of the Severn Gorge was extensively wooded and remained so throughout the industrial revolution, but over the past thousand years the landscape has changed continuously in more subtle ways. The Domesday Book of 1086 describes a landscape of wood pasture, i.e. open woodland where animals, principally cattle, could graze. During the twelfth and thirteenth centuries the land was under the jurisdiction of Forest Law — the Forest of Mount Gilbert on the north side of the river, the Forest of Shirlett on the south side. Deer parks were created on both sides of the river, a fragment of which survives in Willey Old Park.

The great medieval landowner was the Cluniac Priory of Much Wenlock. Wenlock Priory owned Madeley on the north side of the river and part of Broseley on the south side. Priors began to exploit the economic potential by clearing woodland to create farms (assarting) and by digging coal, limestone and ironstone. The dissolution of the priory in 1536 and the sale of its estates by the Crown brought in new landowners who accelerated the pace of industrial development. The land in Broseley was purchased by James Clifford, who inherited the remainder of the manor, and who became the first of the prominent coalmasters. Robert Brooke, Speaker in the House of Commons, purchased Madeley manor in 1544 and erected a house known as Madeley Court on the site of an earlier monastic grange (**4**).

Industrial development could not have occurred when it did without the River Severn. During the middle ages the river was also an important source of food. Fish weirs were a common feature, whereby wicker baskets were attached to stakes and acted as fish traps. The weirs usually involved dividing the river into two channels, leaving an island in the middle known as a 'bylet', the negative consequence of which was that they impeded navigation. In 1575 the owners of 28 weirs in Shropshire were ordered to remove or modify them. Of these, seven were between Benthall and Broseley. One of them, owned by James Clifford, was opposite the site where Bedlam Ironworks was built in the eighteenth century — the bylet is visible on early plans of the site (see **8**).

Coal, ironstone and limestone were worked in the middle ages, and throughout the sixteenth century coal became an increasingly significant part of the river trade. The Severn Valley towns such as Shrewsbury, Bridgnorth and Worcester had outgrown their traditional sources of fuel and sought cheap alternatives. The East Shropshire Coalfield was able to meet this demand largely because the River Severn was a cheap means of transport — Broseley coal was cheaper than Black Country coal, for example, solely because conveyance by road was comparatively expensive. The other factor that made coal mining profitable in the Severn Gorge was the comparative ease with which the minerals

4   Madeley Court was the home of Sir Robert Brooke and his descendants after he purchased Madeley Manor in 1544. The great hall was on the left. The ornate porch and the wing on the right were added in the late sixteenth century

could be won. Coal outcropped on the hillsides and could be dug from shallow pits, or could be worked by driving levels into the hillsides (originally known as 'insets', but more commonly known as adits).

It was the south side of the river, in Broseley, Willey and Benthall, where coal was easiest to exploit, that prosperity was achieved first. By the 1590s Broseley coal was sold as far afield as Gloucester and by the end of the seventeenth century it had reached Bristol and the ports of north Somerset and Devon. In 1570 the population of Broseley was a little over 100, but by 1700 it was nearly 2000. Benthall saw growth of similar proportions, its population during the same period rising from about 80 to roughly 500. Broseley had become one of the largest towns in Shropshire: in 1680 it was claimed that the ancient commons were 'in greatest measure built up and enclosed by poor people' and that the village 'has become a country town'. The prosperity of the coal trade was also reflected in the houses of the coalmasters, only a few of which, like Raddle Hall in Broseley, have survived. Bedlam Hall in Madeley Wood was built in the early seventeenth century and appears in two early nineteenth-century paintings (**colour plate 2**, see **23**). The Lloyds was a large timber-framed house of 1621 (see **47**), which survived to the early twentieth century.

Coal mining was a highly capitalised industry, and its development was spearheaded by local landowners, notably James Clifford, who was admonished by the Commissioners of Sewers in 1575 for dumping the spoil from his mines into the Severn. In the seventeenth century the other most prominent coalmasters were John Weld, who owned collieries in Broseley and Willey, and Lawrence Benthall. Mines were also operated by tenants. On the north side of the river difficulties were encountered with mine drainage, although many tenants obtained leases to drive adits and lay rails.

Among the early tenants were Richard Willcox and William Wells, who had obtained a lease to dig for coal and lay rails in Willey, although their railway crossed land owned by James Clifford, their chief rival. Records of two lawsuits, of 1606 and 1608, give us a valuable picture of the operation of the mines. Clifford's men, apparently 'the scummes and dregges of many countries', were accused of damaging the railway laid by Willcox and Wells, who allegedly countered by damaging the rails and pit-head gear belonging to Clifford. The outcome of the dispute is not known, but the episode highlighted the importation of labour to the district. Indeed, the local population resented the immigrant miners Clifford had attracted, who were allowed to build cottages on common land. Clearly a breed apart, one local resident described the miners as 'thieves . . . horible Swearers . . . daillie drunkerds, some havinge towe or three wyves'. The dispute also drew attention to the early use of wooden railways in the coalfield, among the earliest uses anywhere in Britain (see Chapter 6).

The growth of mining fed other trades. Miners needed large quantities of candles, blacksmiths found work shoeing horses and repairing miners' tools, coopers made water barrels for use in the mines, while carpenters shaped pit props and constructed head stocks and wooden railways. In the nineteenth century, wooden baskets on wheels were found in adits that James Clifford had worked in the late sixteenth century (unfortunately the artefacts have since vanished). Barges were also constructed in Madeley and Broseley by 1660 and the second trade of the district after mining was that of the trowmen or watermen. A study of the seventeenth-century male population of Broseley, for example, found that 23% of men were trowmen or watermen, compared to 43% who were miners.

By the mid-seventeenth century limestone was burnt in kilns in Benthall, the burnt lime being shipped down river as far as Worcester and used as fertiliser. In the 1690s tar, pitch and oil were extracted at Jackfield from bituminous shale by a special process patented by Martin Eele. Later, from the 1730s, lead ore mined from Llangynog in Montgomeryshire and Stiperstones in west Shropshire was smelted on the banks of the River Severn using local coal. After coal, the second most versatile mineral was clay. Bricks were a respectable building material from the seventeenth century and were made locally. During the same period tobacco pipes were made in small workshops in Broseley, originally stimulated by the presence locally of good white clays. 1634 is the earliest date claimed for the nascent pottery trade of Jackfield, based on the recovery in the nineteenth century of a mug with the date moulded on it. Until the end of the eighteenth century most local pottery was made in 'mughouses' with small kilns attached to them and was little different from the domestic production of clay pipes (**5**).

The other trade of the Severn Gorge was of course iron. Although ironstone, or 'mine', was found amid the coal measures, coal and iron were separate trades in the seventeenth century, the reverse of what they became a century later. The reason was simple: until the eighteenth century charcoal and not coal was used for smelting iron. In 1536 there was a bloomery at Coalbrookdale and the existence of another at Willey is well attested during

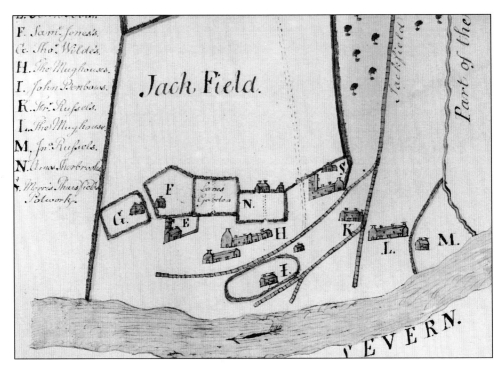

5 *This plan of Jackfield, drawn in the early eighteenth century, shows the small mughouses with kilns attached to them. The tracks are wooden railways from the Broseley collieries, allowing coal to be conveyed to the River Severn*

the same period. Known as the 'direct process', a bloomery was a bowl-shaped furnace packed with layers of crushed ore and charcoal where the ore was heated slowly and then hammered to remove impurities, the eventual product of which was a pure, malleable iron. Its successor was the 'indirect process', which emerged gradually in medieval Europe from taller and narrower bloomery hearths known as shaft furnaces. Here the iron remained in contact with the fuel for a longer period, allowing iron to combine with carbon and to melt at a lower temperature (1150C) than pure iron (1540C). The molten iron that was tapped from the furnace had a carbon content of 3–4%. It could be cast into moulds (cast iron) or allowed to form long bars (pig iron) ready for further refining. The heat of the furnace was maintained by the constant operation of bellows — hence the term blast furnace – that were invariably powered by waterwheels.

Blast furnaces existed in Sweden from the early middle ages, and reached full development in Italy by the fifteenth century. The earliest English blast furnace was built at Newbridge in the Weald in 1496. The earliest blast furnace in the Severn Gorge was built c1618 at Willey, after John Weld had purchased the manor. Weld charged his furnace with iron-rich waste from the former bloomery. In the 1630s another blast furnace was built at Leighton, 4 miles (6 km) upstream from Ironbridge. A blast furnace was also built at Coalbrookdale in 1658. From the blast furnace pig iron was sold on to forges for

6 *The timber-framed Rose Cottages in Coalbrookdale stood next to Basil Brooke's steelworks, established in the early seventeenth century*

refining into wrought iron, and from there wrought iron bars (known as bar iron) were sold on to craftsmen at smithies, or 'secondary forges', where finished products were manufactured, principally horseshoes, tools, locks and nails.

The development of the iron industry, like the coal industry, was dependent upon capital investment, with the local landowners leading the way. Basil Brooke of Madeley patented a process of steel-making and had a steel works in Coalbrookdale, which shipped steel goods down the River Severn from about 1615–1680. Steel is an alloy of iron, which contains a small proportion of carbon (up to 1.5%), necessary to harden the edges of tools. In basic terms, Brooke's method required wrought iron wares to be heated in a charcoal hearth for a considerable length of time, up to three days, a process known as cementation.

In the late seventeenth century the iron trade of the Severn Gorge was no larger or more significant than any other district of Shropshire or the Black Country. Furnaces for smelting were to be found where ironstone could be exploited and where there was adequate water to supply a waterwheel. Charcoal, however, was often transported considerable distances to a blast furnace. Forges relied principally on an adequate water supply for the waterwheels and were much more evenly spread over rural Shropshire. Between furnaces and forges there was a busy trade in semi-finished goods, forgemasters buying pig iron that suited their specific needs.

A survey of the British wrought iron trade made in 1717–18 suggested that the forges in Coalbrookdale were at that time the least productive of all the Shropshire forges. These figures concealed, however, the central role of Coalbrookdale in the imminent and unprecedented development of the iron industry. Investment in ironmaking at Coalbrookdale had been considerable in the second half of the seventeenth century. The works were spread out by the need to exploit the water supply to the maximum extent, and a series of pools provided water to work the wheels. The blast furnace was erected in 1658 and was at the upper end of the Dale. Further down were a series of forges, including the Upper Forge where wrought iron was made from as early as 1668, Basil Brooke's steelworks, next to which workmen's cottages were built in 1642 (**6**), and the Lower Forge, a secondary forge where in 1660 William Hallen and John Spencer were making frying pans. The early history of the Coalbrookdale blast furnace is obscure, but in 1696 it was leased to Shadrach Fox. Fox abandoned smelting, however, after the furnace was damaged by a flood that took place c1705. The furnace remained idle until Abraham Darby came from Bristol in 1708 to found an iron and brass works.

3
IRON

Abraham Darby I is a pivotal figure in the history of the industrial revolution, whose influence was to alter the economic and industrial geography of Britain. His short career was polarised around two places, linked by the River Severn. From his Bristol and Coalbrookdale foundries came innovations that were to revolutionise the iron industry and which remain the basis of iron and steel production today. Darby was born in 1678 near Dudley into a family of farmer-craftsmen, typical Black Country people who worked in an iron forge on a seasonal basis and farmed to supplement their income. He was first apprenticed to a maltster and fellow Quaker in Birmingham; then in about 1700 he moved to Bristol, where he was involved in a variety of enterprises, but principally a brass works and a foundry casting iron cooking pots. The technology he learned in these trades he was to take to Coalbrookdale and apply to the iron industry. For example, in Birmingham he had been introduced to coke, which was used in the drying of the malt, and in Bristol he learned that coal and coke could be employed successfully in the smelting of copper and melting of brass.

In 1703 Darby established an iron pot foundry in Cheese Lane, Bristol, buying pig iron from the Forest of Dean. It was probably his ambition to control his own source of iron that subsequently led him to Coalbrookdale. Here he intended to operate his own blast furnace and to apply fossil fuels to both iron and brass founding. In 1709 the furnace at Coalbrookdale was in blast again and Darby successfully smelted iron ore with mineral fuel for the first time. It had not been possible to use coal because it contained sulphur that would have contaminated the iron. Coking the coal, whereby the coal was smouldered to drive off impurities, removed the sulphur.

His initial success was shortlived, however, as the quantity and quality of his iron left much to be desired. To remedy this he tried various sorts of coal, even having it shipped in from far away ports such as Bristol and Neath. Ultimately he found the local 'clod coal', hitherto deemed the lowest quality of Shropshire coal, to be the most suitable and his iron-making business slowly took a turn for the better. His copper smelting and brass-founding business at Coalbrookdale did not prosper, however, and most of the equipment was shipped back to Bristol in 1714.

The advantage of coke over charcoal was that coal was far more plentiful than wood and it was easier to exploit. It has been estimated that at the end of the seventeenth century one blast furnace fuelled with charcoal required 4200 acres (1700ha) of coppiced woodland to sustain production, but reserves of coal in Ironbridge could support numerous furnaces. The new limiting factor was water, since waterwheels were the only source of power for driving the bellows. In 1715 Darby erected a second blast furnace at Coalbrookdale, using water that had already been harnessed at the old furnace. The furnaces were now known as the Lower and Upper Furnaces, with separate waterwheels to power the bellows and each served by its own reservoir.

Darby's breakthrough did not make an immediate impact on the iron trade and there is no special reason why it should have done. The long-held notion that he rescued the trade from a crisis in the supply of wood has now been largely refuted by historians and archaeologists. In fact there were sufficient renewable sources of wood to sustain national output, which at the end of the seventeenth century was about 29,000 tons of pig iron per year. Coke smelting, which ultimately forced the iron industry away from traditional areas like the Weald and the Forest of Dean to the coalfields, allowed vast increases in overall output. There were still obstacles to be overcome, however, particularly in persuading the forge masters that coke-smelted iron was as good as charcoal pig iron, and in finding an expanded market for iron products.

Abraham Darby's use of coke was one of the most important technological breakthroughs in the industrial revolution. One of the consequences of this is that his other important innovations have often been overlooked. In Bristol he introduced the technique of sand moulding, applying technology that he had learned in the brass trade. Iron was traditionally cast into moulds made of loam, a mixture of sand, clay, straw and manure. Cooking pots cast in this way were crude, while the mould had to be formed every time a casting was made. Darby introduced wooden patterns that could be pressed into boxes of sand, the advantage of which was that more intricate and precise shapes could be cast and, although making the initial patterns was expensive, the patterns could be used again and again to produce identical castings.

He also adopted a special kind of furnace for melting the iron, having found that the quality of the iron was improved if he could remelt it rather than cast it direct from the blast furnace. The air furnace was already used in brass founding. It had two chambers: a firebox for the fuel, usually coal, and a separate hearth, or bowl, for the metal. Heat was drawn from the firebox across the hearth by the draught of a tall chimney (because heat was deflected from the roof of the furnace it was also known as a 'reverberatory furnace'). Separating the fuel and the iron meant that sulphur in the coal would not contaminate the metal. Air furnaces could melt larger quantities of iron than the single tapping of a blast furnace, allowing larger objects to be cast. Furthermore, separating the smelting and the casting processes allowed the ironmasters much more control over production.

By 1715 a new pattern of ironworking had been established at the Upper and Lower Works in Coalbrookdale — the coke-fired blast furnace, attached to which was a foundry with air furnaces (**colour plate 1**). This laid the foundation of the future mass production of cast iron, although it was Darby's successors who reaped the rewards of it. After a lengthy illness, Abraham Darby I died in 1717 at the age of 39. The future management of the ironworks at Coalbrookdale was in doubt for a time because he died intestate. But by the end of the 1720s the works were managed by a partnership which included his son, Abraham Darby II (1711–1763), Thomas Goldney (1664–1731), a Bristol merchant, and Richard Ford (1689–1745).

The second Abraham Darby entered the trade in 1728 and became a full partner ten years later. In the 1730s the partners foresaw an upturn in the demand for iron and

7 *A view over the Coalbrookdale Upper Works by Francois Vivares, dated 1758 and packed with interesting detail. On the left is an engine cylinder being transported from the boring mill further down the Dale. The buildings in the middle include the tall chimneys of two air furnaces and the wider top of the blast furnace belching smoke. To the right is the reservoir for the waterwheels, with the coke hearths in the foreground. In the background beyond the reservoir are Dale House and Rosehill House, with Sunniside further up on the horizon, all ironmasters' houses, and Tea Kettle Row on the side of the hill with its characteristic dormer windows*

exploited it by leasing John Weld's old blast furnace at Willey, on the south side of the River Severn, in 1733. They also had interests in another at Bersham near Wrexham. Like the two Coalbrookdale furnaces, both were fired with coke, these four being the only furnaces where charcoal was successfully superseded until the 1750s. In fact the Shropshire industry continued with its charcoal-fired furnaces, the nearest to Coalbrookdale being at Leighton. Charcoal pig iron was still considered of superior quality to coke iron and coke iron had not been used successfully to make wrought iron. The principal reason for this was the chemical composition of the local iron ores, whose comparatively high levels of phosphorous produced a brittle finished product.

The Coalbrookdale ironworks developed the trade in cast-iron cooking pots, grates and household utensils, the finished products being shipped to the Black Country or Bristol. The most notable products were cylinders for Newcomen steam engines and cannon. Engine cylinders were made at Coalbrookdale from 1722 and until 1733 could only be made under licence as their manufacture was restricted by patent. It was Darby's adoption of both sand moulding and air furnaces that made the casting of large precision items like cylinders possible, although they still had to be bored with revolving cutters (**7**).

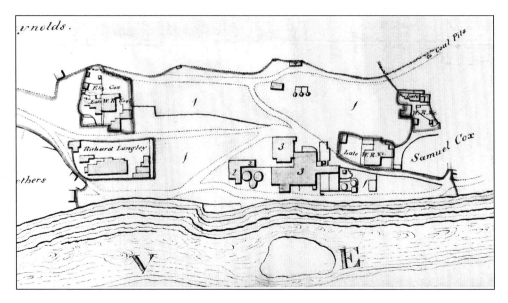

8 *This plan of Bedlam was surveyed for an early nineteenth-century lease of the site. The pair of circles defines the boilers for the pumping engine. The two furnaces, with charging houses and casting houses, are in the centre. To the right (labelled '1') are coke ovens built in 1789, while the hillside above the furnaces was the main coke yard. Upper left is Bedlam Hall, a former charter-master's house converted into tenements, subsequently demolished to make way for a gas works in 1839. The cottages to the left and right are typical examples of haphazard residential development. Note the island in the river: known as a bylet, it denotes the sixteenth-century fish weir on the opposite side of the river to the furnaces*

In 1750 there were three coke-fired blast furnaces in Shropshire but by 1760 there were 12. The sudden growth in the Shropshire iron trade was the dominant part of a national trend. During the 1750s and 1760s many of the most famous British iron companies, such as Carron in Scotland and Dowlais and Cyfarthfa in Wales, were also founded. In 1754 Abraham Darby II leased an expanse of flat featureless land at Horsehay to the north of Coalbrookdale, where two blast furnaces were erected over the next two years. Another site, further north at Ketley near Wellington, was acquired in 1756 for the erection of two more blast furnaces. Neither site was favourably located with regard to water supply, a problem Darby ingeniously solved by adapting the technology of the colliery pumping engine. Steam engines were used to recycle the water used by waterwheels, a method already in use at Coalbrookdale.

During the 1750s other individuals began to make their mark on the local iron trade. In 1757 John Smitheman, who owned a half share in the manor of Madeley, and who had already invested in the development of the local mines, became the major shareholder in the Madeley Wood Furnace Company. The partners erected the two Bedlam Furnaces on the north bank of the River Severn (**8, colour plate 2**). Here an engine was used to pump water from the river to supply the waterwheels. An early plan of the works shows the two blast furnaces with two small air furnaces and moulders' shops, the pattern of iron production which had been developed by Abraham Darby I. In 1757 the old furnace at Willey was taken over by a partnership known as the New Willey Company, who promptly added a second furnace on a new site. The partners included William Ferriday, a partner in the Bedlam Furnaces, and John Wilkinson, an ironmaster from Bersham. William Ferriday was also one of the partners who erected the Lightmoor Furnace, which was established in 1758, north of Coalbrookdale.

The organisation of iron smelting was also changing during this period. Abraham Darby I had purchased his coke and iron ore from local coalmasters, but in the 1750s Abraham Darby II took out leases which granted him the right to extract the ironstone and coal himself. This became the norm: The Madeley Wood Furnace Company, for example, was a partnership in which coal masters predominated, and before building the furnaces at Bedlam it obtained leases for exploiting mineral deposits in a district which soon expanded to become known as the Madeley Field. Ironworks were now large, integrated operations that controlled the whole process of iron making from getting the raw materials to making the finished products.

The 1750s saw coke-fired Shropshire pig iron sold for refining at forges in the Black Country, such as those of the Knight family of Stourbridge. Wrought iron could now be forged from coke pigs by selecting ores that were low in phosphorous, a significant breakthrough that would have consequences nationally. Cast iron, however, became the mainstay of the local trade, and in addition to cannon and parts for steam engines, such varied items as waterwheels and, later on, bridges and other engineering work were produced.

From the 1760s John Wilkinson (1728–1808), whose last will was to be buried in an iron coffin, rivalled the Coalbrookdale partners as the most prominent of the Shropshire ironmasters (**9**). The Wilkinson family was already steeped in the iron trade. His father, Isaac, had been an iron founder in the Lake District but had established himself as an ironmaster at Bersham near Wrexham, also taking shares in the Dowlais and Plymouth works in Merthyr Tydfil. John Wilkinson became a partner in the New Willey works in 1757, apart from which he retained an interest in the ironworks at Bersham, while in 1766 he established a new, larger works at Bradley in Staffordshire. Although not an innovator himself he was quick to apply the ideas of others. In 1774 and 1775 he took out patents for the boring of cannon and engine cylinders which, although they were largely copied from the techniques developed by Jan Verbruggen, a Dutchman, and used at Woolwich Arsenal, allowed the Shropshire ironmasters to develop their business in engines and ordnance.

Wilkinson himself developed a close association with James Watt, who had been granted a patent for his steam engine in 1769, which was to remain in force until 1800. Wilkinson agreed to supply the firm of Boulton and Watt with the precision-bored cylinders they required. In fact only the second Boulton and Watt engine to be built was installed at the Willey ironworks, in 1776, where it was used to blow the blast furnaces directly by means of a large air cylinder. Previously engines had merely circulated water for waterwheels but, by eliminating the need for a waterwheel, the proximity of a water supply would no longer be a requirement for the industry.

9 *The profile of John Wilkinson on one of his trade tokens. Tokens could be exchanged for goods at company shops but at inflated prices. Wilkinson tokens were issued between 1788 and 1795 and the edges were inscribed with the names of his ironworking empire: Willey, Snedshill, Bersham and Bradley*

Wilkinson's new engine worked very well and similar engines were soon installed at Horsehay and Ketley. Blowing engines were also a boon to the new generation of blast furnaces built on the south side of the Severn. At Calcutts, built in the late 1760s, and Benthall, of the late 1770s, engines were initially used to recycle water. But two new works erected in the last two decades of the eighteenth century, Barnetts Leasow (1797) and Coneybury (1786–7), were supplied with blowing engines from the beginning.

It is a common misconception, however, that the steam engine quickly relegated the waterwheel to the realm of the rural corn mill. Recent archaeological work has highlighted the continuing viability of waterwheel technology in the British iron industry well into the nineteenth century. The blast furnaces at Coalbrookdale and Bedlam, for example, continued to be blown from waterwheels. At Coalbrookdale cast iron waterwheels were installed in the 1770s where they were used to power cast iron blowing cylinders rather than bellows. The disadvantage of bellows was that they were large, at least 20ft (6.1m) long, and could only be applied to one side of a furnace. From blowing cylinders, however, blast pipes could be directed to two or three sides of the furnace, thus improving the distribution of the air supply.

During the second half of the eighteenth century there was also a growth in the manufacture of wrought iron in Shropshire, precipitated by the successful forging of coke-smelted pig iron in the Stour valley forges. In the eighteenth century wrought iron was classed into two broad categories: the highest grade was 'tough' iron, made from non-phosphoric ores from the Forest of Dean and Cumberland, and imported in large quantities from Sweden. The coal-measure ironstones produced the more brittle 'cold-short' iron, which was particularly favoured in the nail trade but was less malleable and harder to work than the tough iron. The consequence of this, as far as forging in Coalbrookdale was concerned, was that local pig iron was not always used. Until the 1780s the Coalbrookdale Company's principal forge was the Upper Forge in Coalbrookdale, although it also had a forge in Bridgnorth on the River Severn from 1760. Pig iron for the forge was brought to Coalbrookdale from far afield, sometimes even as far as the American colonies, and different pigs were blended in order to produce bar iron of the required quality.

Not only was pig iron traded like a semi-precious metal, it was also necessary to use charcoal in the refining process. Following the widespread adoption of coke smelting, efforts were made to find a method of making wrought iron with mineral fuel rather than charcoal. If such a method could produce iron of a tolerable quality from coal-measure ironstones, then hitherto untapped reserves of iron ore and coal could be exploited to make iron more economically and more efficiently. From the 1760s competing processes were tried in South Wales, the Midlands, Yorkshire, the Lake District and Scotland. In 1766 Thomas and George Cranage of Coalbrookdale were granted a patent for making wrought iron in an air furnace using coal. Two such furnaces were erected at the Upper Forge, but the process did not work sufficiently well and was abandoned a year or two later. A more successful process was 'stamping and potting', described below, a version of which was patented in 1773 by John Wright and Richard Jesson and was used at several Shropshire ironworks. In addition to their forge at West Bromwich in the Black Country, Wright and Jesson established a forge at Wrens Nest, about three miles south east of Broseley on the River Severn, where an engine was used to recycle water for the wheels driving the hammers. They also built the two blast furnaces at Barnetts Leasow in 1797 and 1801.

The Coalbrookdale Company adopted stamping and potting at the Upper Forge and at Ketley and Horsehay. However, the process reigned only briefly, since it was overtaken by a technique known as puddling and rolling, patented in 1783 and 1784 by Henry Cort of Funtley Iron Mills near Portsmouth. Cort was a former naval bureaucrat and was familiar with the Royal Navy's reluctance to purchase inferior British iron — ships' anchors, for example, were usually forged from high-grade Swedish iron. The Navy had awarded lucrative contracts for British cast iron and Cort foresaw the vast profits that the British forge masters could accrue by making iron acceptable to the Navy Board. Initially, Cort's process was greeted apathetically by the trade — he demonstrated the technique at Ketley in 1784 but could not persuade the Coalbrookdale partners to pay a royalty to use it. But in the 1790s its successful application in Wales catapulted Britain to supremacy in the European iron trade, and also signalled the end of an era for the Shropshire industry.

The heyday of the iron trade in Shropshire was the late eighteenth century, and it was created and sustained by its people. Some of the achievements of the Darbys have already been described, but in fact the ironworking concerns at Coalbrookdale were owned by a partnership of Quakers interrelated through marriage. Richard Reynolds (1735–1816), another Bristol merchant and son-in-law of Abraham Darby II, moved to Shropshire in 1756 and took over the management of the Ketley ironworks (**10**). When his father-in-law died in 1763 he also took on the management of the other Coalbrookdale works until the young Abraham Darby III succeeded in 1773. Reynolds' son was William Reynolds (1758–1803), the most innovative of the Shropshire ironmasters (**colour plate 3**). With Joseph Rathbone, son-in-law of Abraham Darby II, William Reynolds established an ironworks at Donnington Wood north of Coalbrookdale which came into production in 1785. Reynolds also formed a partnership with Joseph Rathbone's son William, who married William Reynolds' sister. In 1794 Reynolds and Rathbone purchased the unprofitable Bedlam works from the Coalbrookdale Company, which had been purchased by Abraham Darby III in 1776. Two years later they acquired the Ketley works when the Coalbrookdale partners effectively divided their empire into two: the Darby family retained the Coalbrookdale and Horsehay works and traded under the name of the Coalbrookdale Company.

The casting of ordnance was lucrative for the iron trade in the late eighteenth century, partly due to Wilkinson's patents for boring cannon but mainly due to the commercial opportunities presented by the Revolutionary and Napoleonic wars with France, 1793–1815. Best known of the cannon foundries was the Calcutts ironworks on the south bank of the Severn, purchased in 1786 by the Scots ironmaster Alexander Brodie (**11**). The New Willey and Benthall works were also notable cannon founders.

John Wilkinson and the Wright and Jesson partnership had interests in both the Shropshire and Black Country iron trades. Such geographically separated interests were common in the eighteenth and nineteenth centuries. William Banks and John Onions, for example, controlled the Coneybury and Benthall ironworks in Shropshire and Brierley in Staffordshire in the late eighteenth century. Onions subsequently had interests in the Donnington Wood and Snedshill blast furnaces in Shropshire. He may be an obscure figure now, but Onions was described as the 'father of the Shropshire iron trade' on his death in 1819.

While the careers of the Shropshire ironmasters have been much praised, far less attention has been given to the furnace, foundry and forge workers, which has led to an unbalanced view of the trade with the masters as the heroes and the men as the foot soldiers. The reality was quite different. Iron making in the eighteenth and nineteenth centuries was a highly skilled operation that could only be learned by empirical means. These skills were closely guarded by men protecting their trades, with a consequence that our knowledge of the manufacturing processes is not as complete as it might be. In

10 *Richard Reynolds (1735–1816). Although not an innovator himself, Reynolds was the most capable businessman of all the Coalbrookdale partners*

11 *The Calcutts Ironworks in 1788. Calcutts was famous for casting ordnance during the war-torn decades of the late eighteenth and early nineteenth centuries. The furnaces and their smoke dominate the picture, but on the right is a small corn mill*

a modern steel works, the processes are automated and chemical analysis is used to assess the quality of the finished product. In the Shropshire iron trade, quality was judged by an experienced eye and motive power was largely provided by manual labour.

When Abraham Darby I adopted coke smelting the iron trade was small enough for him to take a hands-on role, but he would necessarily have had to rely on local experience about the operation of a blast furnace. As the trade developed the ironmasters grew more remote from the actual working practices. For example, when Henry Cort demonstrated puddling at Ketley in 1784 it was not William Reynolds who vouchsafed the quality of the iron produced, but his forgemen: although the ironmasters brokered new technology, they were not themselves the masters of it.

The operation of an ironworks involved many skilled workers and always an army of labourers to assist them. The most skilled or physically demanding jobs were a male preserve; women and children were employed in what were then regarded as light duties. Wage levels in the industry are not always easy to pin down because figures sometimes hide the wages paid out to helpers, but the furnace keepers and forgemen earned the highest wages as the most skilled men. In the 1790s Joseph Plymley found that some ironworkers earned as much as £2 per week, but labourers in the industry were paid a mere 11–12 shillings, only 1–2 shillings more than could be earned in farm work.

The raw materials for the blast furnaces — iron ore, coke and limestone — required varying degrees of preparation for the furnace. Limestone acted as a flux during smelting.

It was used untreated, although it had to be broken up into lumps down to the size of an apple. Iron ore was brought to the works along the networks of wooden railways and plateways. Alternatively, and even in the heyday of the Shropshire iron trade, some iron ore was imported from the Lake District. Ores were first roasted, or 'calcined', to remove some of the impurities. During the nineteenth century, special calcining kilns came into common use, but the traditional Shropshire method had been to calcine the ore in open heaps. On to a bed of coals about 10in (0.25m) deep the iron ore was piled to a depth of 4-5ft (1.2-1.5m), work quite likely to have been undertaken by women, girls and boys working for the mine-burner. Once it had been fired the pile was covered with coal dust to reduce the amount of oxygen to the fire, thus allowing the iron ore to be smouldered over a lengthy period. The time it took to calcine the iron varied between several hours and about three days. Calcining kilns were similar to lime kilns: a kiln was charged from the top with alternate layers of coal and ironstone and, after burning in oxygen-starved conditions, the roasted ore was 'drawn' from the bottom. The optimum size for a piece of ironstone for the furnace was about the size of a man's fist.

Coal was coked in a similar way: the usual Midlands method was to burn coal slowly in open heaps of up to 18ft (5.5m) diameter. Often the coal was heaped around a circular brick turret that helped to control the flow of air, a technique that survived into the early twentieth century at Blists Hill (12). Women, girls and boys were often employed to prepare the heaps and were at the same time employed to carry the coke to the furnaces. To damp down the flames, the coal was covered with earth and ashes, or straw and tree bark, although if the wind whipped through the smouldering heaps then it would burst suddenly into a sheet of flame. The length of time that coking took again varied according to the quality of the coal; contemporary accounts vary from six hours to two days.

A blast furnace was charged at the top and tapped at the bottom, and so there were always two working levels at a furnace site. The raw materials were assembled in a charging house at the top of the furnace. In the eighteenth century raw materials were tipped in to the furnace manually from baskets, but these were subsequently replaced by wheeled barrows. Quantities of ironstone and limestone were often weighed before charging, but coke was judged by eye. Charging of the furnace was continuous and one of the most unhealthy jobs in the industry, given that furnaces gave off quantities of carbon monoxide. The charging house, a warm and sheltered place throughout the year, also became a popular impromptu meeting place, a role which not all ironmasters tolerated. The Coalbrookdale Company, for example, occasionally remonstrated against the presence of 'idle and disorderly people' disrupting the work of the fillers.

The proportions of raw materials depended on a number of factors, such as the quality of the iron ore and coke, and whether pig iron was required for casting or forging. Visitors to Coalbrookdale in the late eighteenth century gave different amounts. In 1785 the La Rochefoucauld brothers saw the blast furnaces at Coalbrookdale charged with eight baskets of ore to five of coke and three of limestone; in 1796 Joshua Gilpin saw a ratio of 7:2:1. At Ketley in 1803 Simon Goodrich saw a ratio of 13:5:5.

The furnace keeper determined the make-up of the charge. To manipulate a 30ft high furnace reaching temperatures of 1500C, and constantly blown with air from a giant cylinder, required a good deal of subtlety in order to make it yield iron of the required

12 *Coke hearths at the Blists Hill Ironworks in the late nineteenth century. Coal was heaped up around the brick tunnels, which acted as a draught while the coal was being burnt*

quality. In 1815 the Yorkshire ironmaster Thomas Butler visited the Bedlam furnaces, which had an established reputation for producing high-quality pig iron for the foundry. Butler was told that their blast furnaces only made 25 tons of iron per week, but that if lower quality forge pigs were required the furnaces could make 35 tons. In order to make iron of the highest quality, it was also necessary that the air was blown into the furnace at a steady but not brutal velocity.

The interior of a blast furnace was designed with three main components (**13**). At the bottom was the hearth, usually circular and with a straight wall, near the top of which the air was blown through one or more tuyères (tuyère is French for pipe); above it were the boshes which fanned out to the maximum width of the furnace; above the boshes was the stack which narrowed all the way up to the tunnel head, which acted as a chimney to carry the fumes above the charging level but was also where the furnace was charged. Inside the furnace the raw materials gradually sank down through the stack to the boshes, which was the melting zone. From here the molten iron and the waste, known as slag, dripped down into the hearth. Slag was lighter than iron and floated on top. Therefore whenever the furnace was tapped the slag was drawn off first. The skill of the furnace keeper was in judging the quality of slag in its molten state, since by this means he could judge the

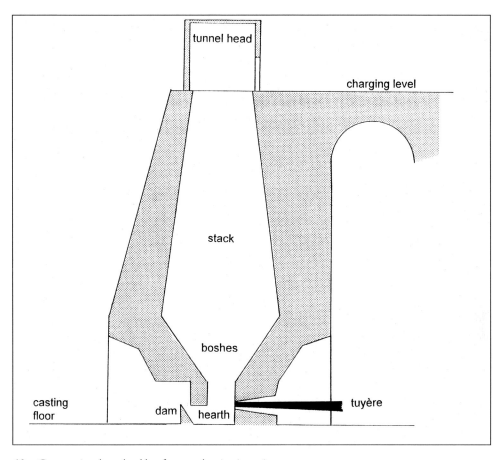

13 *Cross-section through a blast furnace, showing its main components*

quality of his iron. If the slag was too fluid more iron ore was needed, but if it was viscous then more limestone was needed.

Once a furnace was in blast, smelting was a continuous operation. Although it was possible to refrain from blowing the furnace for a few hours a week to allow maintenance work to take place, if a furnace was allowed to cool its lining would crack. Before a steam engine for recycling water was constructed at Coalbrookdale in 1743 there was insufficient water for smelting to be a year-round operation. Instead the furnace was worked in 'campaigns' over the winter months, after which essential maintenance was necessary once it had cooled.

An idea of the number of people employed in the operation of a blast furnace is given by a comparison of the number of workers employed on a campaign at Coalbrookdale and continuous smelting at Bedlam. In 1709, when Abraham Darby introduced coke firing at Coalbrookdale, the workmen were Richard Beard, the mine-burner, Richard Knowls, who stocked the charging house with raw materials, Richard Hart, the filler, John Felton, the furnace keeper and John Tyler, the founder.

In 1794, when William Reynolds gained control of the Bedlam works and only a single furnace was in blast, the account book lists 20 people employed at the blast furnace, with two additional men tending the pumping engine that supplied water to the waterwheel. The presence of two furnace keepers, Richard Sides and Richard Key, shows that two 12-hour shifts were in operation. Only one of the employees listed, Elizabeth Hilling, was female, and she was engaged with three others as a filler. Materials preparation was the responsibility of three men — Robert Cox, the mine-burner, Richard Hart, coking and John Hill, limestone breaker — with others employed to stack the ore and clean the mine bank. Richard Sides' son was the blacksmith's boy.

The daily division of labour into two shifts was dictated by the need to tap the furnace every 12 hours. Meanwhile the necessity of maintaining the furnaces in blast meant seven-day weeks. Night crews saw little daylight while their two-week shift lasted. The change from night to day work was the most gruelling aspect of employment at the blast furnaces because it meant working a 'double turn' of 24 hours. In the early nineteenth century it was remedied in part by letting the furnaces 'stand' on a Sunday. This was introduced at Bedlam about 1815, and was copied by the Coalbrookdale Company and other works in the Shropshire Coalfield.

When a furnace was tapped the molten iron could either be cast into moulds or run into sand beds as pig iron to be sent for further refining. Work in the foundries and forges was less relentless than it was at the blast furnaces. By the end of the eighteenth century, only coarse items such as floor plates or water pipes were cast direct from the blast furnace. It was more common to melt pig iron either in an air furnace, or in a more modern 'cupola' furnace. Cupolas were invented by William Wilkinson and were patented in 1794 by his brother John. They are tall shaft furnaces blown with a tuyère, and charged from the top and tapped from the bottom, much like a blast furnace. They are still used in foundries today. Pig iron for the foundry varied in quality depending on the proportion of trace elements such as phosphorous and silicon, and the proportion of carbon. Variations in the fluidity of the iron, caused by the amount of carbon, rendered some brands most suitable for fine, precision items, while more viscous iron suited purposes where strength and durability were required. The pig iron from Bedlam, for example, belonged to the latter category and was known as 'grey-melting'.

While the pig or scrap iron was in the air or cupola furnace the moulds were made up by the moulder. These were made from patterns of brass or hardwood in the manner developed by Abraham Darby I in the early eighteenth century. Many founders employed boys to assist in the fetching and carrying. The tapping of the furnace was accompanied by a procedure that remains familiar from foundries across the world. The following account was written by Joshua Gilpin on his visit to Coalbrookdale in 1796:

> When ye workmen hear the bell each moulder from the various rooms runs with a ladle of iron to catch a due quantity of metal & takes it to his mould which he fills with it — a mould is always to be filled at one pouring; if one man's ladle will not hold enough at a time a large one is brought carried by two or more persons & if a very large casting, the metal is run into a large pot & both hoisted & carried to the mould by a Crane.

A visitor in 1801 remarked that in the foundry at the Lower Works in Coalbrookdale there were six cranes and several ovens for drying the moulds. He also noted the characteristic 'pop' of the casting boxes caused by the expansion of air within the moulds once they had been filled.

The most interesting products of the local foundries, from a technical point of view, were cannon and engine cylinders, since both were sent to boring mills for finishing. At Alexander Brodie's Calcutts works in 1796, Charles Hatchett saw one air furnace cast two 32-pounders at a single tapping. Six years later the Swedish metallurgist Svedenstierna was told that they could cast excellent quality cannon direct from the blast furnace as long as 'the charge and the blast are adapted accordingly'. Hatchett then saw the boring mill at Calcutts where up to eight cannon could be bored simultaneously. Power was supplied by a single steam engine that turned the blades of the boring mechanisms. These were fixed with hard steel cutters. Each cannon was fixed to a rack which, by means of weights, was advanced upon the boring mechanism, thus allowing the blades to work slowly through the shaft of the cannon.

The manufacture of engine cylinders was a similar process and the same precision techniques were also applied to making pump barrels for the drainage of the mines, whereby water was raised in the barrels by suction. Simon Goodrich, a naval engineer, gave a detailed description in 1803 of the Coalbrookdale Company's boring mill at Coalbrookdale, situated downstream from the blast furnaces. Here a waterwheel 19ft (5.8m) in diameter turned the boring mechanism, which Goodrich estimated made no more than one revolution per minute as it was advanced upon a large cylinder 78in (2m) in diameter. At the Coalbrookdale Upper Works he found a turning mill where the exterior surfaces of the cylinders were smoothed and polished, and a second mill where the pump barrels were bored.

Two earlier visitors, the La Rochefoucauld brothers, were particularly impressed with boring techniques, which they saw at Coalbrookdale and Wilkinson's Willey Ironworks in 1785. Their description of casting and boring cylinders and pump barrels conveys something of the range of precision products manufactured in the foundries and the kudos the workforce derived from their specialist skills:

> The best workmen are put on to make [the engine cylinders]: the difficulty comes with matching them up when they are finished. However, they work with such precision that they even cast the great cogwheels, with teeth fitting exactly into those of another wheel made alongside it, and there is never a shortage of such products ... We saw many [cylinders] of considerable size that they have lately produced. We admired them as things simply unknown in our country: they smiled, and when I asked them which piece they found the most difficult to cast, they replied that nothing they did was difficult.

These skills were no less real for being elusive 200 years later, but the rub was the physical stamina required for any such work in a foundry or forge. The La Rochefoucauld brothers perceptively noted of the workmen that 'they scarce ever live to old age: they eat and drink everything they earn and are miserable all their days'.

The ability to make wrought iron from pig iron was widely accepted as the most difficult of all the metallurgical trades. Until the latter part of the eighteenth century wrought iron was generally made in a finery and chafery. The finery was constructed like a typical blacksmith's hearth, but larger and fanned by much bigger bellows. Fuel was invariably charcoal until coal and coke were introduced in the mid to late eighteenth century. Pig iron was broken up and thrown into the fire. The job of the finer was to stir the iron with a long bar and to bring it into contact with the blast of air from the bellows. The chemical process involved in fining was simple. Pig iron contains 3-4% carbon, but if it was heated to a high enough temperature and brought into contact with air then the carbon would react with the oxygen to form carbon monoxide and leave the iron in a pure, malleable state.

Once this had been achieved the iron was removed with large tongs and placed under a large hammer. The hammer beat the iron, known as a 'bloom', into shape and at the same time expelled all the waste, known as 'slag' or 'dross'. The process was known as shingling and it was well known that repeated hammering improved the quality of the iron in much the same way that kneading improves the quality of bread. In fact hammering was the most effective method of judging the quality of the iron — if the iron contained too much sulphur, for example, it was known as 'red-short' and shattered under the hammer blows. Fining and shingling were undertaken at least twice before the iron was sent to a second hearth, known as the chafery, where it was re-heated sufficient to be hammered again. The iron was now hammered, or 'drawn' into bars up to 10ft (3.05m) long, in which state it was sold to secondary forges for making nails, screws, pans and the like. Nails were made at the Lower Forge in Coalbrookdale, where frying pans were also produced in the seventeenth and eighteenth centuries (**14**). In 1789, the 13 Coalbrookdale pan shops were sold and converted into dwellings.

Only two descriptions of the stamping and potting method have survived, both written by French spies — Marchant de la Houlière in West Bromwich in 1774 and the La Rochefoucauld brothers in Coalbrookdale in 1785. Pig iron was broken up and placed in a coke-fired finery, after which it was shingled in the traditional way. However, the hammer was used beat the iron into a flat plate which, after it had been left to cool, was broken up into small pieces using a sledgehammer (stamping). The fragments were then collected up into pots by women who placed them into an air furnace (potting). Inside the air furnace, the iron fragments coalesced and gradually the pots broke up in the heat. According to the La Rochefoucauld brothers: '20 [pots] usually go in at a time: they stay there two and a half hours, while the action of the fire raises the iron to fusion point though it remains solid all the time. The coal has vanished: so have the pots, entirely. The workman inspects it from time to time to see whether the iron is ready: his judgement is the only rule.'

Puddling was introduced at Ketley in 1796, followed by Horsehay in 1798. It was never adopted at Coalbrookdale or any other ironworks in the Ironbridge district. Several visitors witnessed its use elsewhere at the turn of the nineteenth century, however. The basic principle of the technique was that iron was stirred in an air furnace to produce a bloom that was hammered in the traditional way. After a second heating the iron was passed through a rolling mill rather than being formed into bars under a hammer. It was much quicker and cheaper than stamping and potting although it did not achieve one of

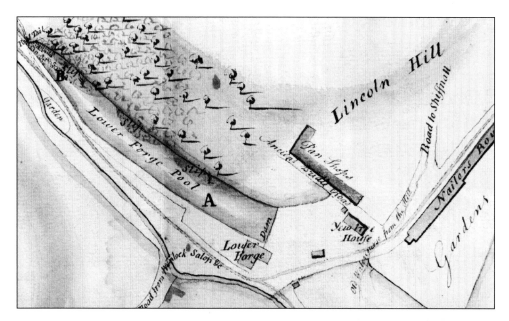

14 *The Lower Forge at Coalbrookdale, surveyed in 1786. The pan shops were disused only three years later. Note Nailers Row and the vegetable plots indicated in front of them. Part of the pan shop range, as well as Yew Tree House, are all that survives to the present day*

the other aims of the ironmasters, to undermine the arcane mysteries of the forgeman's craft. Puddlers were the aristocrats of the iron trade and had to be paid accordingly.

Puddling did not immediately supersede stamping and potting. In fact at Ketley and Horsehay a combination of both methods was in use for a time. When Simon Goodrich went to Coalbrookdale in 1803 he found stamping and potting still in use at the Upper Forge, where he was told that the iron was of better quality than the puddled iron though not as cheap. Stamped iron was known as 'best hammered iron'; it tended to be harder than puddled iron and was particularly favoured by nail makers. At Horsehay stamped iron was generally used for making boiler plates.

The effect of puddling in the early nineteenth century was to alter the dynamic of the British iron industry. To make it commercially viable, rows of puddling furnaces were required with large banks of rolling mills, the consequence of which was that ironmasters needed larger, flatter sites to erect new ironworks on an unprecedented scale. The ironworks in the Severn Gorge, like the Upper Forge at Coalbrookdale, or the Calcutts and Barnetts Leasow works on the south side of the River Severn, could not erect such large works because the topography was unsuitable. Nor could the raw materials be extracted in the same volume and at the same economy as in places like Staffordshire and South Wales.

At the beginning of the French wars in 1793, the ironworks of the Severn Gorge were at the forefront of technology and spearheaded an economic district of some importance. When peace came in 1815, it had lost its technological supremacy and had become an

15 *The Blists Hill blast furnaces, painted in 1847 by Warington Smyth. The engine house on the left was built in 1832 but was replaced in 1873. The distinctive shape of the furnaces, like a pottery kiln, was a local characteristic*

outlier of an economic district centred on the Black Country around Wolverhampton. After war ended there was a slump in the demand for iron that saw both of the Coalbrookdale blast furnaces blown out. They were probably never used again. The Bedlam furnaces were also idle in 1817. Worse was to happen at Ketley, when the proprietors decided to cut their losses and close the works. The bitterness that this engendered was remembered by John Randall who, writing in the late 1870s, expressed the distress and anger felt in the neighbourhood that followed the euphoria of Waterloo:

> With glorious victory came fearful collapse, and the country awoke to find a fallacy which it had been taught to regard as truth — that war brings commercial advantages that compensate for fearful waste and lavish expenditure . . . Iron from £18 had gone down to £7 per ton, paid from Ketley to Stourport. Mr Reynolds believed the trade would never again rally, and resolved to blow out the furnaces at Ketley. This was in 1817. In 1818, at an immense sacrifice of property, consisting of the usual apparatus for making and manufacturing iron, he sold off at an immense loss, and removed to Bristol. Language cannot paint the deep distress which accompanied and followed this.

16 *The Coalbrookdale Company's Lower Works, and principal foundry, in the mid-nineteenth century. The warehouse behind with the clock tower is now the Coalbrookdale Museum of Iron*

But the Ketley works did open again and the Shropshire trade recovered as the nation's iron trade recovered in the 1820s, although by now the geography of the local industry was quite different. The ironworks on the south side of the River Severn closed first, although most of them died slowly and had no formal date of closure. Calcutts was out of production by 1815, Barnetts Leasow, Broseley and Benthall Furnaces by 1821, Willey by 1830. The two works on the north side of the river — Coalbrookdale and Madeley Wood — survived by adapting themselves to changed economic circumstances.

In the 1820s the Coalbrookdale Company concentrated their smelting operations on Horsehay and a new works at Dawley Castle, north of Coalbrookdale, which came into production in 1810. In 1839 the company also purchased the old Lightmoor Ironworks. Bedlam Furnaces, which after William Reynolds' death in 1803 passed to his nephew, William Anstice, and operated as the Madeley Wood Company, concentrated on pig iron production, the Crawstone ores from the local mines enabling the company to make foundry iron of wide repute. In 1832 the company built a new furnace at Blists Hill, one mile east of Bedlam and on a site which the company owned rather than leased (**15**).

Amid the closures of works south of the river, a new generation of ironworks sprang up on the north side of the Shropshire Coalfield, away from the Ironbridge district, which ceased to be the centre of local ironmaking. The Coalbrookdale Company was nevertheless to enhance its reputation, having integrated the Upper and Lower Works into a foundry where pig iron was melted in cupolas and where specialist products were cast (**16**).

The market for cast iron enlarged and diversified in Victorian Britain and its colonies. The improvements in communications and the invention of the cupola furnace meant

17 *The Great Exhibition of 1851 was a showcase of British industry. Here, from the exhibition catalogue, are a cast iron gate screen and a 'boy and swan' fountain cast by the Coalbrookdale Company*

that large foundries could now operate successfully in any large town. In order to compete and flourish the Coalbrookdale Company needed to specialise, which it duly did. Coalbrookdale now became known for its ornamental cast iron, in particular statuary and gates. The Great Exhibition of 1851 was a triumph for Coalbrookdale cast iron, a success it repeated at other trade exhibitions in the nineteenth century (**17**). It was the trade in cast iron that became the mainstay of the company, the old works at Horsehay and Dawley Castle, and the acquired Lightmoor works all having closed in the later nineteenth century. The Coalbrookdale Company became part of Allied Ironfounders in 1929 and later a part of Glynwed Foundries, a national conglomerate.

The Madeley Wood Company blew out the last working furnace at Bedlam in 1843 but continued to smelt iron at Blists Hill into the twentieth century. By the early nineteenth century the company was principally concerned with coal mining and it is doubtful that iron smelting was profitable by the end of the century. In fact in 1900 only one of the Blists Hill blast furnaces remained in use, by which time all the other Shropshire blast furnaces had been abandoned, except for a modern steelworks at Priorslee, where steel was produced until 1959. In 1800 a blast furnace had been a familiar sight in the district; after 1900 it was a novelty. Many local people, whose memories were recorded in the 1980s, remembered the thrill they had on a Sunday afternoon when they would rush from Sunday School and make for the blast furnace at Blists Hill, which was always tapped at 4 o'clock in the afternoon. Smelting ended in 1912 in the wake of a colliers' strike (**18**).

18 *Ironworkers standing in front of the cast houses at Blists Hill in the late nineteenth century*

The Madeley Wood Company pig iron was a specialist product used for making cast iron objects. In 1828 James Nielson of Glasgow patented a new technique whereby hot rather than cold air was blown into a blast furnace. Hot blast substantially reduced the amount of fuel necessary to smelt iron ore, and consequently allowed new works in Scotland to become significant players in the iron trade. Two Shropshire ironworks, The Madeley Wood Company's Blists Hill and the Lilleshall Company's Lodge furnaces, continued to produce cold blast iron long after Nielson's patent expired in 1842. This was not old fashioned but a case of specialisation, since it was well known that cold blast pig iron made a higher quality cast iron than hot blast pigs. The Madeley Wood Company's principal clients were heavy engineering concerns and the major railway companies. The ultimate reason for Shropshire's reputation for cast over wrought iron, however, was the chance factor of the local ironstone. And the most fitting monument to the local iron trade was, of course, the Iron Bridge across the River Severn.

4
THE IRON BRIDGE: THE 'WONDER OF THE WORLD'

Abraham Darby III was born in 1750 and gained control of the Coalbrookdale Company in 1773 at the age of 23. Before his thirtieth birthday he had made a name for himself on a number of ambitious projects, although none were particularly distinguished business ventures. In 1774 he attempted to buy a 3/8 share in the manor of Madeley that would have made him landlord of his own works. In 1776 he purchased the rival Bedlam ironworks, together with the mineral reserves of the Madeley Field. Archaeology has shown that he also rebuilt much of the Coalbrookdale Upper Works, having his name inscribed on one of the lintels of the blast furnace, built a new mill for producing iron rods at the Upper Forge, and perhaps also rebuilt the Lower Works as well. His other achievement of the 1770s was his biggest financial flop, but in every other respect the Iron Bridge was a technological and cultural triumph that was justifiably described by Viscount Torrington in 1784 as 'one of the wonders of the world'. Although it would be unfair to attribute all the success to a single person, Darby built the bridge and was the driving force behind the project. Indeed, without his determination it may never have been built at all, and it was Darby who bore the heaviest financial burden for its construction.

The idea of a bridge across the Severn between what were then Madeley Wood and Broseley was an obvious one. Both were prosperous industrial districts with a healthy cross-river trade and yet the only links between them were by ferry across a volatile and hazardous river. The nearest bridge was a mile upstream of modern Ironbridge at Buildwas.

The Iron Bridge was conceived by Thomas Farnolls Pritchard (1723–77), who first suggested the idea in 1773 in a letter to John Wilkinson. Pritchard was a well-known Shrewsbury architect, much of whose work can still be appreciated. In Shrewsbury, he built St Julian's church (now a craft centre) in 1749–50 and the Foundling Hospital (now part of Shrewsbury School) in 1760. In the immediate vicinity, he remodelled The Lawns in Broseley, home of John Wilkinson, and built a folly in the garden of Broseley Hall. He had also earned himself a reputation as a designer of bridges. He built a stone bridge across the River Teme at Bringewood near Ludlow in 1772, and in 1773 he began work on a bridge at Stourport in Worcestershire, the new town at the interchange between the River Severn and the Staffordshire & Worcestershire Canal. The bridge, completed in 1775, was a brick structure on an iron frame.

Pritchard intended from the outset that his Madeley bridge should be of cast iron. The initial design had a span of 120ft (36.6m) and was estimated to cost a total of £3200.

Shareholders were sought to raise the necessary capital, which in 1775 yielded a little over £3000, the money to be recouped by charging a toll to cross the bridge. At the first shareholders' meeting, Abraham Darby agreed to act as treasurer and to build the bridge and its approach roads. The other shareholders all had business interests in the locality. Apart from Pritchard, Wilkinson and Darby, Edward Blakeway held financial interests in the pottery and iron industries (and is best known as co-founder of the Coalport Chinaworks); the Reverend Edward Harries was a landowner from Benthall and a noted agricultural improver; Thomas Addenbrooke was a local solicitor; Charles Guest was a merchant and one of the famous Guests of the iron trade; John Thursfield of Benthall Hall was one of the family of potters who dominated the trade on the south side of the river in the eighteenth century.

In order to construct a bridge across the Severn it was necessary to obtain an Act of Parliament. To this end a petition was presented on 5 February 1776 and excited interest from the outset — the Prime Minister, Lord North, requested that drawings for the bridge be displayed in the House. The bill passed through its first and second readings and its committee stages with only minor amendments, and Royal Assent was granted on 25 March 1776. Its relatively smooth passage through Parliament was, however, followed by protracted delays during which time the project nearly floundered. Two factions had emerged among the shareholders: on one side, Darby, Wilkinson and Pritchard advocated an iron bridge; the remaining shareholders lost their nerve and wanted a more traditional design.

It was from this stage onwards that Darby dominated events. He was in a strong position as the principal shareholder, more so when Wilkinson agreed to sell him his own shares, but it was not until October 1777 that new shares were issued and building could go ahead. Meanwhile the design of the bridge had been modified. Pritchard died in December 1777 after a lengthy illness, but there is little doubt that he rather than Darby was responsible for the alterations, as he produced further drawings and a model, for which he received posthumous payment. The new design had a slightly shorter span, of 100ft, 6in (30.2m), and had a distinctive profile, similar to his Bringewood bridge, which would allow a Severn trow to pass beneath it without lowering its mast. Construction work began in late 1777 and during 1778 the foundations and stone abutments were built. The cast iron ribs were erected across the river in 1779.

Little else is known about the actual construction of the bridge, a subject that has understandably attracted interest and speculation. For example, it is not known in which foundry the bridge was cast and how Darby secured the necessary quantity of iron. One argument is that Darby purchased Bedlam furnaces in 1776 because he needed the extra ironmaking capacity for the bridge, while another argument assumes that Darby's rebuilding of the blast furnace at the Coalbrookdale Upper Works in 1777 signalled the beginning of smelting for the bridge parts. Neither theory has recognised that Bedlam and the rebuilding in Coalbrookdale were part of Darby's wider ambitions, but the problem of supply must surely have been a real one. The bridge is estimated to have consumed 378 tons of cast iron when a Shropshire blast furnace could produce a mere 20-25 tons of pig iron a week. However, Darby already had two furnaces at Coalbrookdale, three at Ketley and two at Horsehay at his disposal before he purchased the two Bedlam furnaces.

Together they could have supplied enough pig iron over a period of time or through surplus stocks. If any more was required, the easiest and simplest method of acquiring the additional iron would have been to buy it on the open market. Ironmasters regularly traded pig iron with their rivals throughout the industrial revolution. The significance of Bedlam in this is rather dubious. Although it is not known how much the iron for the bridge eventually cost, the iron for Pritchard's initial design, of a longer span, was estimated at £2100. Viewed in this light, the purchase of Bedlam for £4600 would have been an absurd way of making up the difference.

The largest of the cast iron ribs weighed over 5 tons, so they could not have been cast direct from a blast furnace. Instead, the pig iron was remelted in one or more air furnaces and then cast into open sand moulds. The work is most likely to have been undertaken at the Upper or Lower Works in Coalbrookdale, the company's principal foundries, which is certainly how visitors such as the La Rochefoucauld brothers understood it in 1785, and Charles Hatchett in 1796. The Coalbrookdale moulders were used to casting precision items and probably found the bridge challenging but not necessarily daunting. In 1776, for example, they cast two 20ft (6.1m) diameter flywheels for a slitting mill at the Coalbrookdale Upper Forge. For the workmen who had to erect the bridge, however, it was a prodigious achievement to assemble the parts and erect them in a little over three months, and without any of the serious injuries or fatalities that regularly marred such audacious technological achievements.

The total cost of building the bridge is not known. The original estimate allowed £550 for erecting the bridge, but in the event building costs soared to £2373. Rumour that Darby was seriously out of pocket for his efforts were in circulation by the early 1780s.

The year 1780 was spent in building the approach roads to the bridge, which opened officially on New Year's Day, 1781. It was immediately hailed as a triumph and its fame quickly spread across Europe and America — in 1786 Thomas Jefferson obtained an engraving of it which he hung in the White House. The potential of cast iron to achieve both strength and elegance had been demonstrated beyond doubt and by the end of the eighteenth century replicas had been built at Raincy near Paris and at Worlitz near Magdeburg in Prussia. Britain embraced the possibilities of cast iron ahead of other nations, to such an extent that the technology of the Iron Bridge was soon surpassed. For example, in 1796 Thomas Telford erected a new iron bridge across the River Severn at Buildwas, cast in Coalbrookdale. Whereas the Iron Bridge had required 378 tons of iron, Buildwas Bridge weighed only 170 tons (the bridge suffered from the instability of the river banks and was replaced in 1905–6). Cast iron was also adopted for buildings: in 1796 a cast iron frame was used to construct a flax mill for Charles Bage at Ditherington in Shrewsbury. Thomas Telford was soon to use iron for a canal aqueduct at Longdon-on-Tern near Shrewsbury, and for Pontcysyllte aqueduct on the Ellesmere Canal, which opened in 1805.

The international fame of the Iron Bridge was to a significant extent the product of vigorous promotion by its shareholders. In truth it was not the world's first iron bridge, but it was certainly the first iron bridge worth talking about and worth taking the trouble to visit. In 1780, before it had opened, Darby paid William Williams 10 guineas to paint the bridge, with the intention of having it engraved and published as a print (cover). Williams

19 *The Iron Bridge, after Michael Angelo Rooker. Abraham Darby III commissioned the view in 1780 and a version of it was dedicated to George III*

portrayed it with a carriage crossing it, and a gentleman midstream pointing out its features to two well-dressed ladies. Darby also commissioned a view of it from Michael Angelo Rooker (1743–1801), a scene painter from the Haymarket Theatre in London, which was subsequently engraved and was on sale by 1781 (**19**). Another edition of the print was published by the Coalbrookdale Company in 1782 and dedicated to George III.

The efforts of the shareholders in promoting traffic across the bridge were largely successful. Darby may have been out of pocket, and remained in a difficult financial state until his death in 1789, but he had undeniably created the phenomenon of the age. In the *Shrewsbury Chronicle* in 1786, a London to Shrewsbury stage coach was advertised as passing 'that striking specimen of Art and so much admired object of travellers'. Visitors were many and the praise was effusive. As Samuel Butler wrote in 1782: 'The Bridge itself makes a light & elegant appearance tho' apparently no ways deficient in strength. In viewing it either up or down water it resembles an elegant Arch in some elegant Cathedral' (**20**).

The Iron Bridge had a wider contemporary context as the focus of the district's picturesque scenery and as a symbol of technological endeavour (**21**). Local inns were not slow to advertise their proximity to 'the Manufactories in Coalbrookdale', which were in the vanguard of the revolution in the material world. Ironbridge became a tourist attraction to complement the mountains of Snowdonia and the scenery of the Wye Valley (**colour plate 4**). Contemporary accounts in both words and pictures are valuable contributions to a period in British culture when attitudes to the natural world, science and industry, and the relationships between them, were changing markedly.

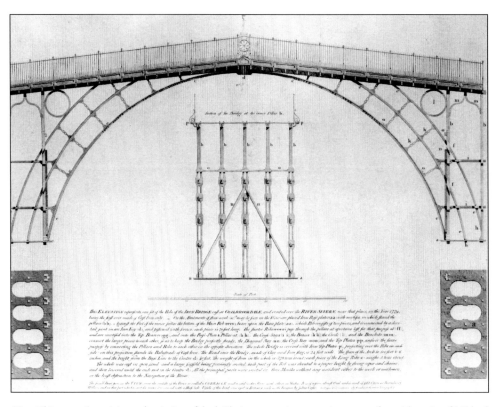

20 *This engraving, giving a description of the bridge's construction, was given away free with copies of Michael Angelo Rooker's engraving of the bridge*

It is a modern misconception that the blast furnaces produced smoke and fumes enough to lay waste to nature in the Gorge. In fact, the district was always well wooded, as can be seen from many contemporary views and accounts, and yet not every one was at ease here. Charles Dibdin, a dramatist and songwriter, recalled a visit in about 1787 when the atmosphere was 'insufferably hot'. He felt stifled by 'the prodigious piles of coal burning to coke, the furnaces, the forges, and the other tremendous objects emitting fire and smoke to an immense extent, together with the intolerable stench of the sulphur'. Richard Colt Hoare, of Stourhead in Wiltshire, complained in 1801 that the solitude of the woods in Coalbrookdale was interrupted 'by the repeated strokes of the hammer in the [forge] beneath'. He did, however, comment that a 'roaring explosion' from the cannon foundry at Calcutts 'produced a fine effect', a typical sentiment during the war with Revolutionary France.

Responses to the landscape of industry varied, not least between its owners and visitors. Richard Reynolds, owner of the Madeley manor from 1781, manipulated the natural scenery as if it was a landscape garden. Atop the steep hill on the east side of Coalbrookdale he laid out two 'Sabbath Walks', ostensibly for the benefit of the workmen.

21 *Engraved after one of George Robertson's views of the district and published in 1788, this print depicts the dramatic landscape setting of the Iron Bridge in the Severn Gorge*

One of them followed a path through woodland to a Doric temple (**22**); the other followed the ridge to a Rotunda perched above Lincoln Hill quarries and overlooking the river. At the Coalbrookdale Upper Works, pleasure grounds were laid out on the banks of the reservoir, with an ornamental iron bridge crossing the end of it (see **48**). At the opposite end of the reservoir were the sulphurous coke hearths.

Ironmasters were also responsible for a burgeoning interest in natural phenomena, especially the study of geology, since mining yielded copious amounts of fossils. In 1751 Richard Pococke, Bishop of Ossory and Meath in Ireland, was shown the collection of one of the daughters of Richard Ford. He was told that it was common to find large reeds, tree bark and fir cones in the ironstone beds. George Perry also noted an 'Abundance of Fossil Shells and Corals' from the limestone quarries. William Reynolds too was a noted collector of fossils, as erudite on the subject of geology as on so many other things.

Visitors responded to the landscape in their own way. Contemporary attitudes to industry in the Severn Gorge were quite different to that of our own generation and changed noticeably during the eighteenth century and again in the nineteenth century. In

22   *The Doric temple was one of the two ornamental buildings constructed by Richard Reynolds along his Sabbath Walks on the hilltop above Coalbrookdale*

the mid-eighteenth century, the watchwords were productivity and a harmony between nature and industry. Writing in 1758, George Perry described Coalbrookdale as 'a fine fertile Country, Water'd by the Severn', its beauty enhanced by 'Pillars of Flame and smoke rising to a vast height, large Reservoirs of Water, and a number of Engines in motion, [which] never fail to raise the Admiration of strangers'. Indeed, Coalbrookdale was one of the 'few Places where rural prospects, and Scenes of Hurry and Business are so happily united'.

By the end of the eighteenth century the emphasis shifted from passive to more dramatic responses. Aesthetic approaches to nature and industry were also overlain with patriotic sentiments during hostilities with France between 1793 and 1815. A shift in the concerns of artists is demonstrated by comparing two views of Coalbrookdale created in 1758 and 1777. The earlier is an engraving made by Francois Vivares showing the group of buildings at the Upper Works, people engaged in various activities and an engine cylinder in transit from the Coalbrookdale boring mill (see **7**). The scene is of a busy and productive world. Nearly twenty years later, William Williams set the Coalbrookdale iron industry in a scene of pastoral beauty. The distant smoking furnaces stand oddly in the midst of it, however, while the figures in the foreground live in a different world and look away from the furnaces as if they were not there (**colour plate 5**). In 1776 Arthur Young, an agricultural journalist, expressed similar misgivings by describing Coalbrookdale as composed of 'beautiful sheets of hanging wood', and yet 'too beautiful to be much in unison with that variety of horrors . . . the noise of the forges, mills, & c. with all their vast machinery'. Indeed 'the flames bursting from the furnaces with the burning of the coal and the smoak of the lime kilns, are altogether sublime'. In a similar vein of discord between nature and industry, Anna Seward's poem The Swan of Lichfield, written about 1785, describes the 'woodwild glens' of Coalbrookdale as a pastoral idyll. But in the violated glens:

> . . . Pond'rous engines clang
> Through thy coy dales; while red the countless fires,
> With umber'd flames, bicker on all thy hills
> Dark'ning the Summer's sun with columns large
> Of thick, sulphureous smoke

Anna Seward's ambivalence to industrial scenery was typical of her time. She was horrified by it, but at the same time she found it exhilarating and was struck with a sense of the vastness and power of machines and furnaces. The visual equivalent of this response was most famously portrayed by the artist Philip James de Loutherbourg (1740–1812).

De Loutherbourg was a well-known purveyor of hot-blooded and patriotic images, and he visited Shropshire to make sketches for his *Picturesque and Romantic Scenery of England and Wales*, published in 1805 (**colour plate 6**). His best-known image, however, is the painting of 1801, misleadingly titled Coalbrookdale by Night (the scene is the Bedlam Furnaces in Madeley Wood), which exudes the same vastness, power and pyrotechnics that Anna Seward described (**23**). De Loutherbourg's picture has become particularly well known since its acquisition by the Science Museum in 1952.

23 *'Coalbrookdale by Night' by Philip James de Loutherbourg, first exhibited in 1801. The scene is Bedlam Furnaces, with Bedlam Hall on the left. Although de Loutherbourg made numerous sketches of local scenes his finished painting is largely a product of the imagination*

It has graced more book covers than any other image of the industrial revolution and has become an unofficial symbol of the period. Coalbrookdale by Night is classic de Loutherbourg, but the substance of the picture is actually rather shallow. The landscape is suitably blasted; the foreground rustics are formulaic, while Bedlam Hall, the seventeenth-century house on the left of the picture, looks appropriately spooky. De Loutherbourg was a scene painter for the London theatre and was not interested in the technical aspects of iron making. Indeed the engine house and smithy of the furnaces, at the bottom right, look a little like farm buildings although they are portrayed reasonably faithfully. The impact of the picture is provided by the light in the sky, derived from the coke heaps in the centre of the picture that would periodically burst into flame, lighting up the night sky if a gust of wind passed through them. The furnaces themselves are nowhere to be seen.

This sublime industrial landscape was also the scene of numerous technological innovations. Among them were the inclined planes connected with the collieries and the Shropshire Canal (see Chapter 6) and the china manufactories at Coalport and Caughley that were established at the end of the eighteenth century (see Chapter 7). Some of the inventions of John Wilkinson have already been described, like his boring machines and his association with the Boulton and Watt engine. In 1787 one of his blacksmiths at Willey, John Jones, constructed the first boat with an iron hull. Called the Trial, its first trip was to Birmingham via the River Severn and Birmingham Canal.

The most scientifically accomplished of the local industrialists was William Reynolds, described by his fellow ironmaster Richard Crawshay as 'having more Metalurgie & Chemical Skill than any other of my Friends' (**colour plate 3**). During the 1790s he established the new town of Coalport on the banks of the River Severn, at the interchange between the river and the Shropshire Canal. Here, Reynolds put his considerable energies into developing what might now be classified as an industrial estate. The most famous of the enterprises to be established there was the chinaworks of Blakeway, Rose & Rose, but the others included a pottery, brickworks, a ropeworks supplying rope to Coalbrookdale mines, a timber yard for building tub boats, and two chainworks.

William Reynolds' most ambitious scheme for Coalport was the establishment of a chemical works. The idea had been put forward by his friend Lord Dundonald, an eccentric inventor, the kind of person who gravitated to places like Ironbridge in search of men to put his ideas into practice. Dundonald's capacity for innovation was unfortunately in inverse proportion to his business acumen. He must have cut a peculiar figure travelling around the country incognito, staying in lowly inns to avoid pursuing creditors. But he was a significant creative force whose experiments with coke and tar ovens will receive their share of attention in due course.

The chemicals factory was intended to be an integrated works manufacturing alkali, glass, soap, alum, white lead, dyes and fertiliser. Reynolds was enthusiastic in principle and assured Dundonald that most of the raw materials required for such an enterprise, such as brine, pyrites, iron slag, potash, litharge (lead oxide), sand, tallow and limestone, were available from Reynolds' existing enterprises. A site for the works was apparently chosen somewhere above the river at Coalport. In the event the factory was never built: by 1800 Reynolds' health was failing and he decided to take a break from his business activities. He died in 1803 at the relatively young age of 44. Had he lived longer the history of Ironbridge might have been quite different.

Reynolds also contributed to the development of technology by introducing new innovations at his ironworking and mining enterprises. At the mines he helped to pioneer new technology in steam engines, employing Adam Heslop who made a steam engine to rival that of James Watt. Watt successfully pursued a case that Heslop's engine infringed his own patent, but in the meantime Reynolds had several Heslop engines erected in the Madeley mines for pumping and winding duties, some of which continued to be used into the early twentieth century. Reynolds also purchased engines designed by James Glazebrook, a novel kind of engine because it was not a beam engine (one of which he was planning to install into a pleasure boat). Nor were the engines constructed in Coalbrookdale in 1792-3 by James Sadler, before he embarked on a more illustrious career as a balloonist.

Perhaps the most remarkable of these pioneering engineers was a Cornishman, Richard Trevithick (1771-1833). Trevithick was developing engines that used steam at high pressure. Previously steam had been condensed in cylinders to create a vacuum, thereby forcing the piston down. In 1803 Simon Goodrich saw an experimental engine erected at the Coalbrookdale Upper Works, in which the engine cylinder was placed inside the boiler. One of the advantages of Trevithick's designs was that such an engine, together with its boiler and chimney, was small enough to be mounted on wheels. In other words, Trevithick invented the steam locomotive. His first prototype was a road locomotive that

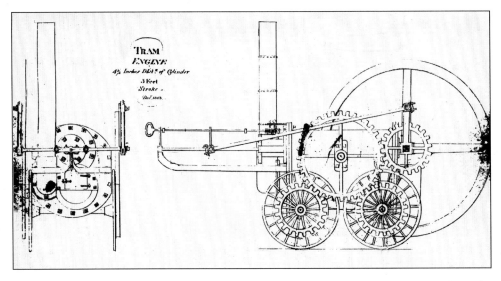

24 *The steam locomotive built by Richard Trevithick in Coalbrookdale in 1802–3. It seems certain that trials were conducted at Coalbrookdale before an identical locomotive made a well-publicised journey in South Wales a year later*

he tried at Camborne in 1800. In 1802–3 he built a locomotive at Coalbrookdale that was designed to travel on rails (**24**). It may have undergone some trials, but glory came a year later when an identical locomotive made a triumphant 12-mile trip down the Taff valley in South Wales.

Trevithick was a long way ahead of his time, but his engines stood at a threshold between two phases of mechanisation in the industrial revolution. Hitherto, steam engines had been heavy, ponderous devices firmly rooted to the ground, but in the nineteenth century they became light and swift machines, epitomising a new era of hurry and business. It was to be over 20 years before George Stephenson's Rocket ran on the Liverpool and Manchester Railway. In the intervening period Ironbridge changed immeasurably and the prevailing attitude to technology and progress experienced a marked downturn, precipitated partly by the gruelling war with France. The chief symbols of this period expressed anxiety that technology had advanced so far as to control human destiny — the Luddite smashing of machinery in the Midlands textile industry in 1811–12 and Mary Shelley's novel *Frankenstein*, first published in 1819. The Iron Bridge was just as potent a symbol, but it characterised the more optimistic world of the eighteenth-century Enlightenment when it seemed that new innovations could only work for the benefit of humankind.

5
RAW MATERIALS

Mining has the longest history of any of the local industries, but has left comparatively little archaeological evidence behind. It may now be the least tangible aspect of the industrial heritage, but exploitation of mineral resources was the basis of industrialisation. Coal was initially worked for the River Severn trade by numerous coalmasters, or 'charter-masters', who moved into the iron trade when the two industries became integrated from the 1750s. Coalmasters were prominent in the partnerships that founded the Bedlam and Lightmoor furnaces in the 1750s. It proved to be a turning point in the industry. In the future, mining was controlled by fewer concerns and output grew to keep pace with the increasing demand for raw materials in the iron industry and the market for sale coal.

Significant advances in mining technology were part and parcel of this development, a consequence not only of the need to increase production but also of having exhausted the most accessible measures. The earliest method of extraction was the mining of surface or shallow deposits by means of circular bell pits, so named because they were wider at the base than at the top. The pits were dug manually to as great an extent as safety would allow, up to 33ft (10m) deep and 15ft (4.5m) wide. The spoil was dumped in a ring around the top, and then a new pit would be dug following the line of the seam. Bell pits therefore were dug in series. In Ironbridge, bell pits were most commonly found south of the River Severn in Benthall and Broseley where the terrain was slightly less precipitous and the coal measures at a shallow depth. The alternative method was to drive adits into the hillsides, which even in the seventeenth century could be extensive operations. In 1649 Edward Cludde obtained a lease allowing him to mine coal in Madeley; two years later four adits had been driven, two 3000ft (915m) long, the others 2100ft (686m) and 1500ft (457m) long respectively.

Coal was extracted from underground by means of the 'longwall' system, which was pioneered in the East Shropshire Coalfield from the seventeenth century onwards and became the principal method of deep mining, more often associated with shafts rather than adits. At the base of the shafts were horizontal roadways leading to the coal seams. These were worked from galleries at right angles to the main roadways. The basic principle was that coal along a face was undermined by 'holers', who cut away the clay beneath the coal seam and built up supports to keep the mass of coal in place. The coal was then cut down by 'pikers'. Once the coal had been removed, the resulting cavity, known as the 'gob', was filled up with rock and waste material and, later, pit props. Ponies were used to haul the coal along the main roadways to the base of the shafts, while boys pulled the coal in sledges where the roofs were otherwise too low.

25 *Horse-powered winding mechanisms, known as horse-gins, were a familiar sight in the eighteenth century as they were the standard method of raising coals from mine shafts until the advent of the winding engine. Note also the wooden railway for conveying coal either to the ironworks or the River Severn*

Mining was greatly aided by the development of steam technology. In the early bell pits, the coal was raised from a shallow depth using a manually operated windlass. In deeper mines, a horse gin was used, whereby a winding cable was wound around a drum turned by a horse (**25**). Steam engines were initially used for draining water. The earliest engine in the district, or indeed anywhere in Shropshire, was erected in the Lloyds in 1719, only seven years after the first recorded application of a steam engine to drainage work. The engine was replaced in 1745 when John Smitheman erected a new engine to stimulate further exploitation of Madeley Wood's mineral reserves, the sale from which provided him with a royalty as lord of the Manor (**26**). In 1768 two visitors to the area were told that the Coalbrookdale Company operated six pumping engines at its own mines.

The application of steam technology to turning a winding drum did not occur until the late eighteenth century when the vertical motion of the engine was transferred to a rotative motion by means of gears and crankshafts (**27**). William Reynolds pioneered the use of winding engines, employing Adam Heslop to construct engines for the Madeley Wood mines in the last decade of the eighteenth century (**colour plate 7**).

Employment in the mines was grim, dangerous and exhausting. The educated classes were horrified by what they knew of life underground, and although their emotionally

26 *The Lloyds Engine House was built in 1745 and a succession of engines housed in it pumped water from the coal levels until 1914. The beam can be seen protruding from the building above the pump shaft. On the left is a winding mechanism used for lifting the pump rods from the shaft*

27 *This primitive engine, in use at one of the Coalbrookdale Company's pits at Lightmoor in the late nineteenth century, was one of the earliest to incorporate rotative motion for winding*

charged descriptions often border on the patronising, the conditions they wrote about were real enough. The Methodist minister John Fletcher sets the scene: 'Destructive damps, and clouds of noxious dust, infect the air they breathe. Sometimes water incessantly distils on their naked bodies; or bursting upon them in streams, drowns them and deluges their work.' As the geologist Joseph Prestwich noted in the 1840s, 'when the seam is very thin they will have to work lying on their sides'. And as one Shropshire coalmaster observed of his employees in 1835, 'few or none escape accidents', while another observed that about 10% of accidents were fatal. Frequent causes of death were rock falls, a characteristic hazard of the longwall system, and accidents while ascending or descending the shafts, caused by a number of factors — the breakage of ropes or cables, the cages swinging out of control in the shafts, or the winding engines failing to stop when the cages reached the top or bottom. No wonder when John Randall went down a mine in the 1850s he noticed that 'a group of pit girls and boys share a sly joke at your expense'.

Randall has given us one of the most vivid descriptions of the strange underground environment, written after visiting one of the collieries in Madeley Wood in the 1850s. As the basket descends the shaft:

> You feel to be standing on a column of thin vapour, that now assails your nostrils with mingled smells, as down, down goes the skip on which you stand, and you

follow by virtue of your own weight. Drops of water patter on your head, coal dust fills your eyes; the ascending loads shoot upwards, and soon a glimmering light from the bottom points out the limit of your descent . . . You have a candle, stuck into a bit of moist clay — a very convenient candlestick, too, for a mine, seeing that you can fasten it to the side or anywhere you like. With this, your eyes having become accustomed to the gloom, you can now explore the mine. You pass the stables, which in a pit have a curious indescribable smell. You observe the roof bulging in and bending down the cross-timbers that rest on stout upright 'trees' for support. Here and there, it may be, are hollows where, having been disturbed by older works in strata a storey higher up, it has fallen in, forming dark caverns, in which explosive gas accumulates. Touch it with a candle and it will flash like gun-cotton, in blue flames along the roof. A door, kept by a boy who sits all day pent up in darkness to perform this monotonous duty, opens to admit us. We come across boys . . . drawing coals or 'spoil' to the wagons. These appear like imps; while the men, naked to the waist, toiling in deep twilight and black coal-dust, wielding picks and maundrels, look full-grown demons. The atmosphere is oppressive, and you perspire freely as you find yourself in the inner recesses of the mine.

The organisation of labour in the mines was hierarchical. The process of getting the coal was organised by charter-masters, or 'butties', who were sub-contractors to the coal-owning companies. The charter-master agreed to raise a given quantity of coal at a pre-determined price, but was not responsible for sinking the shafts or draining them. The charter-masters hired the workforce to labour underground. Their most skilled workers were the holers and pikemen, usually combined into a single role during the nineteenth century, who commanded the highest wages. Colliers generally worked 12-hour shifts and an 11-day fortnight. Alternate Saturdays were called Reckonings, when the workforce was paid. Many of the charter-masters owned public houses or truck shops. The truck system, whereby tokens could only be exchanged for goods at inflated prices, was notoriously exploitative and declined in the nineteenth century, although the charter-master system survived into the twentieth century in Shropshire.

Relatively high wages were the inducements offered to compensate for the dangers of the occupation. In 1776 Arthur Young noted that a collier's wage was about 18s 4d for a fortnight, which compared favourably with work at the foundries and potteries, and was significantly higher than the wages paid to agricultural workers. Pit boys drawing coal baskets could earn in the region of £14 a year, compared with £2 on a farm. Boys were employed to work on menial tasks underground from the age of about six, usually pulling sledges from the face to the main underground railways, or opening and closing the air doors, a system designed to control ventilation. The worst excesses were probably dying out when the Children's Employment Commission inspected Britain's industrial districts in 1842, looking for evidence that legislation was needed to curb child labour. But few people who entered the mining trade moved out of it. When the coal measures around Broseley were worked out in the 1820s, there was emigration to the newer mining districts rather than a shift to other, less dangerous jobs.

28 *Miners at Blists Hill Pit in the late nineteenth century, when red clay was mined for the neighbouring brickworks. The winding engine in the background was built by Adam Heslop in the late eighteenth century. The pit ponies were experiencing a real treat, as they were rarely brought up to the surface*

Parallel with coal mining was ironstone and clay mining. These minerals could be extracted from the same pits as coal, although it was unusual for them to be exploited concurrently. Usually the clay was extracted after the coal had been worked out, assuming that suitable veins could be found for specific purposes. Ironstone, also known as 'mine', was extracted in the same manner as coal, except that more work was required on the surface. When the 'mine' was brought up to the surface, the nodules of ironstone were mixed up with clays and shales. The material was dumped onto the pit banks and teams of girls were employed to pick out the ironstone by hand. The nodules were transferred to baskets, which the girls traditionally carried on their heads to the heaps of ironstone, ready for despatch to the ironworks. Girls were employed on the pit banks usually from their early teens until their early twenties. In the 1840s this could still be regarded as healthy work since, although it was carried out in all weathers, the atmosphere was far more refreshing than life underground. In other respects it was unskilled and undesirable; local girls with greater aptitude found opportunities for skilled work at the potteries and the Coalport Chinaworks. The women worked in teams and, during May, they left Shropshire for three-months' work in the market gardens around London, where they were a familiar sight selling vegetables and strawberries at market. It was comparatively lucrative work and allowed them to save up a dowry or find work in domestic service in London.

In the late eighteenth century there were two significant by-products of coal mining — the extraction of natural bitumen and the manufacture of coke in ovens, which yielded coal tar as a by-product. The tar tunnel near Coalport was cut in 1786 and was conceived as a means of access between the Blists Hill Pits and the River Severn. Instead, the tar that oozed from its walls was tapped and sold in a refined condition as British Oil for medicinal purposes, or was boiled into pitch. In 1787 the tar spring yielded 55 gallons per week, which at a cost of 16 shillings per barrel could in theory have brought William Reynolds a considerable income of £2288 a year. In 1796 Joshua Gilpin went 3300ft (1006m) into the tunnel and saw preparation for linking it with the Madeley mines, for which it acted as a ventilation and drainage outlet.

The commercial manufacture of coke was pioneered by Archibald Cochrane, the ninth Earl of Dundonald. Dundonald's work is of special interest as a precursor of what was to become a common industry in British coalfields in the nineteenth and twentieth centuries. His first coke ovens were erected on the south side of the river at the Calcutts in 1784. More kilns were built at the Benthall ironworks in 1787 but were discontinued a decade later. Coal was burnt in ovens, from which the smoke was drawn into a funnel covered with water. The coolness of the water condensed the smoke, leaving tar to form in the bottom of the funnel. The tar was sold in London, where some of it was used for an experimental internal combustion engine, while the pitch derived from it was used for caulking ships. The kilns at Calcutts were evidently successful, as a second bank was erected between 1799 and 1803 — an early nineteenth-century plan of the site shows 20 kilns. Before Dundonald, coke ovens had been erected at the Bedlam Furnaces, although they were disbanded by Abraham Darby III in about 1779. Later, Dundonald persuaded William Reynolds to resurrect the idea and, in 1789, two new coke ovens were erected at Bedlam.

The other major extractive industry was the quarrying and mining of limestone. Numerous small quarries were worked in the Benthall area and limestone was taken down to the riverside by means of a railway inclined plane. Here, some was taken to local blast furnaces — in 1756 limestone was ferried across the river to the Horsehay blast furnaces of the Coalbrookdale partners. Most of it, however, was burnt in lime kilns. A large bank of kilns was built close to the river in Benthall, served by railway from the quarries. Burnt lime was used for two main purposes — for fertiliser or for the mortar used in the building trade.

On the opposite side of the river were the vast limestone workings at Lincoln Hill in Coalbrookdale. The workings here were prodigious and attracted awe-struck visitors and fossil collectors. In 1758 George Perry described Lincoln Hill as 'a long tract of hill . . . cut hollow to a great depth, so that the top of it now looks like a vast pit, 440 yards long and 52 wide, each side being a frightful precipice'. The quarries also contained caverns and adits, while at the base of the hill lime kilns were built (**29**), from where the burnt lime was conveyed down the hill to nearby Ludcroft Wharf by means of a self-acting inclined plane. Limestone for the Coalbrookdale and Bedlam furnaces came from here in the late eighteenth century, but the operation of the lime workings was independent of the iron-making partnerships. Limestone for the local blast furnaces was also obtained from further afield, the most common source being quarries on Wenlock Edge.

29 *Lime kilns at Lincoln Hill, sketched in 1802 by Paul Sandby Munn*

The decline of mining in the district was a slow and staged affair. Coal reserves first became exhausted on the south side of the river in Broseley, causing the ironworks to close between 1815 and 1830, but ironstone was still mined and shipped to the Staffordshire ironworks, while clay was exploited for local brick and tile works. For example, in the 1820s the Stourbridge ironmaster James Foster took over ironstone mines previously worked for the Barnetts Leasow and Calcutts furnaces, which were still worked as late as 1879. Foster owned several ironworks, including the Madeley Court Works where blast furnaces were built in 1843, but his Broseley minerals were exported to his Black Country works.

On the north side of the river the mining operations of both the Coalbrookdale Company and the Madeley Wood Company expanded northwards in the nineteenth century, where there were deeper seams to be exploited. By the end of the century the principal mines in the Ironbridge district were those of the Madeley Wood Company. The company continued to mine ironstone, its high-quality Crawstone, Blackstone and Pinneystone ores giving the Blists Hill works its reputation for high-quality foundry iron, but after 1886 its reserves of Crawstone, the best of the ores, had been worked out.

Despite its interests in the iron and brick industries, coal was the core of the Madeley Wood Company's business and investment was made in the deeper mines north of the Severn Gorge near Madeley. The older mines continued to be worked, however, and were renowned for their antiquated equipment. In 1871, the Iron and Steel Institute visited the district and commented upon the old engines with wooden beams used for winding, some of which were designed in the last decade of the eighteenth century by Adam Heslop. In 1912 an American visitor wrote another astonished description of the same engines, one of which was erected at the Blists Hill Pit, close to the ironworks and opposite the company's brickworks. It had been opened in the late eighteenth century, but after 1879 the coal was worked out and a vein of red clay was mined from it for the brickworks. This had happened at other company pits. The most notable was Styches Pit, on the hillside north of Bedlam Furnaces, where a vein of fireclay was discovered in 1841 which warranted the construction of a brickworks at Bedlam. Later its reserves of red clay were exploited for the Blists Hill brickworks. The pit closed in 1912.

Mining in the Madeley Wood area was dependent upon the pumping engine in the Lloyds (see **26**). It continued working until the outbreak of the Great War in 1914, but once it had ceased pumping the levels that it drained could no longer be worked. Indeed during the Great War the working pits of the Madeley Wood Company were beyond the Gorge nearer Madeley town. The Madeley Wood Company continued to mine coal until it vanished under nationalisation in 1947. It was one of the longest established companies in Shropshire and could trace its origins back to the founding of the Madeley Wood Furnace Company in 1756.

6
MOVING THE PRODUCTS

The River Severn was a crucial factor in the industrialisation of East Shropshire (**30**). It remained the principle means of transporting goods — as it had done throughout history — well into the nineteenth century, and was only eclipsed by the coming of the railways. Railway and road networks were national phenomena, but there were other means of transport more specific to the Ironbridge area. Of particular significance were the early wooden railways used to move coal, ironstone and clay to the river wharves, whilst the Shropshire Canal was the subject of a particularly ingenious invention for raising goods from one level to another, the steam-powered inclined plane.

Coal had become an important component of river trade in the sixteenth century and remained the principle export from Broseley and Madeley right through to the mid-nineteenth century. In 1756, it was estimated that over 100,000 tons of coal were shipped from this area each year, along with the products of the iron, lead and ceramics industries. Food, wine, timber and china clay were brought upstream from the ports of Gloucester and Bristol.

The Severn was the second longest navigable river in Britain. Substantial vessels could work the 160 miles from Pool Quay, near Welshpool, all the way to Bristol, although cargoes were frequently transhipped into larger vessels at Gloucester due to the rougher conditions downstream. The main trading vessels on the Severn were barges and trows. Barges were single-masted, up to 60ft (18.3m) in length and could carry up to 40 tons of goods. The wider flat-bottomed trows had two masts and could carry up to 80 tons. When passing under bridges the masts and sails could be lowered. The boats were carried downstream to Gloucester by the current. The return journey was much more difficult (and more expensive) and required the brute force of bowhaulers (**colour plate 4**). In 1756 there were 139 barges and trows belonging to owners in Broseley, Benthall and Madeley, making up a thriving riverside economy. Broseley Wood was where the 'rougher elements lived — bargemen, bowhaulers, waggoners and other river men'. Many subsidiary occupations were also associated with river trading, particularly boat yards (**31**). An Upper Severn trow was found recently at Lydney in Gloucestershire. The wreck was recorded in detail because it was at severe risk of erosion, and was found to be of clinker and carvel construction. It was converted later for sailing on the Lower Severn, where it had to endure estuarine conditions.

Another familiar sight on the river was the coracle. These tiny oval boats had been in use since at least Saxon times, the name coming from the Latin *coria*, meaning leather hides. Although there were regional variations, those in Shropshire were made of narrow ash laths covered by horse-hides and were light enough to be portable on land. A single

30 *In this early nineteenth-century view of the River Severn, looking from the Hay Inclined Plane across Madeley Wood, the crowded, industrialised riverside scene is well portrayed, hemmed in by the gorge*

paddle and a certain amount of skill were required to manoeuvre them. They were used primarily for fishing, particularly salmon fishing, but were also used for short journeys or to get from one side of the river to the other. Boats of all types could be used as ferries, an essential service as there were no bridges between Buildwas and Bridgnorth until 1780. Some ferries were operated by attaching the top of the mast to a fixed rope or iron chain.

Despite the critical importance of the river to the economy of East Shropshire, it was by no means a perfect mode of transport. Archdeacon Plymley wrote in 1803 that 'the navigation is very much impeded by lowness in summer and by floods in winter'. Normally there were several months of the year when the waters were too low for navigation. This situation was thought to have been made worse by the draining of meadows further north in Shropshire. Various schemes were put forward to improve the navigation by deepening shallows and constructing locks and weirs, but these never materialised due to the opposition of the boatmen, who did not want to pay tolls, and the local people who preferred the river in its natural state. The only improvement was the formation of a horse towing path between Bewdley and Coalbrookdale, a scheme put forward by Richard Reynolds, and constructed in 1800. The use of horses to pull boats upstream rather than bowhaulers was widely approved because bowhauling was very much frowned upon as a trade (**colour plate 4**). It was said to be 'injurious to their manners' as well as to their health. Malpractice and trickery were apparently rife amongst the river men. Weight tickets for coal were doctored, whilst upstream groceries and wines

31 *A view across the River Severn from Coalbrookdale to Bower Yard, painted by an unknown but obviously amateur artist in the nineteenth century. On the opposite bank is a boat yard*

had a tendency to disappear *en route*, along with a few fowl and a little game poached along the river banks. The ironmasters were more careful with their cargoes of iron due to its high value, and generally chartered boats. For a short time the Coalbrookdale Company had its own fleet, but for the most part river trade was controlled by the bargemen.

The steepness of the Severn Gorge led to some ingenuity on the part of early colliers, who built inclined railways leading down from their mines to the river wharves. The earliest mention of rails and 'gins' occurs in the colliery dispute in Broseley of 1606–8. Gins were horse-powered winding mechanisms that let down the wagons on ropes. One of the witnesses reported that 'the said engin would by all likelihode have conveyed to the said River . . . more coales in a day than a wayne and 6 oxen were able to convey . . . in 3 or 4 days'. The rails were made of wood and a fragment of a similar railway was found by archaeologists adjacent to Bedlam Furnaces in 1986.

The next critical step in railway technology was the coming of iron: the first iron railway wheels were cast at Coalbrookdale in 1729 for a master collier. Iron rails were introduced by Richard Reynolds at the Coalbrookdale Company's Horsehay works. They were laid on an existing wooden railway from the Upper Works in Coalbrookdale to the River Severn in 1767–8, and were then extended north to Horsehay and Ketley. Only 1.25in (32mm) thick, they were designed to be nailed onto wooden rails and were hence known as edge rails. By 1770, 800 tons of iron rails had been cast. A subsequent improvement was the invention of L-section plateway rails by John Curr, locally known as jinny rails. It was claimed in 1799 that they would halve the cost of transporting coal and iron ore to the furnaces at Coalbrookdale. The wagons on these railways were pulled by horses, but counter-balanced inclines, where the weight of a fully-loaded wagon descending would raise an empty wagon, were coming into use in the mid-eighteenth century. One of these was described by Samuel Simpson at the Madeley mines in 1746: 'A large Barrel or Wind is fixt at the Top, on which runs a large Chain; at each End of this is a Wooden Waggon that will hold about 2 Tons each. This chain reaches to the River; and when one Waggon is loaded at the Top, it sets a going Gradually, which brings the empty one up, and so continues till the Vessel is laden.'

The scope of the River Severn for navigation much increased in the eighteenth century with the development of a national canal network. Shropshire was now linked with the Rivers Dee and Mersey via the Ellesmere, Shropshire and Shrewsbury Canals. At Coalport, there was an interchange between the River Severn and the Shropshire Canal. To the south, another interchange was created between the Severn and the Staffordshire & Worcestershire Canal at Stourport — Shropshire iron could now be exported to Birmingham and the Black Country much more easily. Nearer Gloucester on the Severn, canal links provided access to the River Thames and finally London.

The Shropshire Canal passed from north to south through the East Shropshire Coalfield before reaching Coalport. Many of the principal shareholders of the canal company were local ironmasters who wanted an easy route for the transportation of their products to the River Severn navigation. It was no ordinary canal because of the uneven topography and the difficulty in procuring water. Thomas Telford noted that a canal had been considered impractical for some years before it was built, because it was 'lying on the range which is considered as nearly the highest ground in the kingdom; this ground being also very rugged and consisting of ridges which are insulated from the adjoining country'.

The Shropshire Canal Company was formed by an Act of Parliament in 1788 and construction work began in the same year. The canal was nearly 11 miles long and the specification stated that it was to be 4ft, 6in (1.4m) deep and 16ft (4.9m) wide at its base. Major engineering works were required to overcome the differences in height along its route, and it was realised that locks would not be feasible due to lack of water. The company decided to hold a competition which it advertised as follows: 'A reward of 50 guineas be offered . . . to that person who shall discover and communicate . . . the best means of raising and lowering heavy weights from one navigation to another'. A panel of judges was appointed which included James Watt and John Wilkinson. The joint winners were Henry Williams of Ketley and John Lowdon of Snedshill (**32**). Henry Williams was to become principal engineer and manager of the canal, a post he held for the next 50 years. The double-tracked incline was to have a winding mechanism and loading bays at the top, next to which was a steam engine of the type made by Adam Heslop. A short counter-plane ran into the upper canal basin, and there was another basin at the base of the incline.

The canal inclined planes worked on much the same basis as the railway inclines discussed above. One of the pioneers was William Reynolds, who had built a counter-balanced inclined plane in 1788 on the Ketley Canal for his Ketley ironworks (**colour**

32 *A drawing by Thomas Telford of the inclines on the Shropshire and Shrewsbury Canals. The engines were designed by Adam Heslop, an early rival to Boulton and Watt, and are recognisable because they have a cylinder at both ends of the beam. The layout of engine and winding mechanism shown here was in use at the Hay Inclined Plane*

plate 3). He was aware of other such developments in the country, such as the inclined planes on Ducart's Canal in County Tyrone, which were used intermittently from 1777–87 to take coal to Coalisland. The Shropshire Canal, however, was the first place where steam engines were applied to canal inclined planes.

From Donnington Wood at the north end of the coalfield, where a short canal linked with the Shrewsbury Canal, the Shropshire Canal crossed the coalfield and split into two branches at the south end, one leading to Coalport, the other to Coalbrookdale. The canal-river interchange at Coalport was dominated by an enormous warehouse, which straddled the canal and projected out into the river, so that goods could be taken directly from one to the other (**colour plate 8**). The western branch was to pass through Horsehay and Coalbrookdale and then down to the River Severn, but the last section was not built and the canal terminated just above Coalbrookdale. There were three inclined planes on the eastern branch. Two planned for the western branch were on the section that was never built, but an experimental device was installed at Brierly Hill, just above Coalbrookdale. This was known as a tunnel and shaft system and was described in 1791 by Samborne Palmer, a Somerset collier. Crates were raised and lowered in two parallel vertical shafts by counter-balancing. A large winding drum and flywheel were situated between the heads of the shafts. At the bottom, the crates were loaded into horse-drawn railway wagons in a tunnel 984ft (300m) long. The system did not prove to be a success, possibly because the weight of goods descending was too great, and it was replaced by an inclined railway.

Although the canal was fully opened in 1792, the inclines were probably worked by horses until the engines were finished in 1793. Problems occurred with the canal from the beginning. Pumping engines had been used to fill it with water, but these were removed soon afterwards, and water shortages ensued. Land slips and breaches meant costly repairs and payment of damages to neighbouring land owners. Some slips were caused by natural geological faults, whilst others were the result of mining subsidence.

The ropes at the Windmill Farm and Hay inclined planes were replaced by wrought iron chain in 1800. This was an important technological advance though not without teething problems as the chain would occasionally break. According to John Randall:

> On a chain snapping we have known a canal boat with 5 tons of iron pigs on board gain such velocity that on coming in contact with the water in the lower canal it has broken away from the iron chains which held it to the carriage, bounded into the air, clearing two other boats moored on the side, together with the embankment, and lighted in the Severn, close to the ferry-boat, into which it pitched some of the pigs it contained.

By the mid-nineteenth century the Shropshire Canal was the subject of hostile take-over bids by the expanding railway companies, and it was purchased by the London and North Western Railway in 1857 for £52,000. The last section of the canal from the foot of the Windmill Farm incline to Coalport was by-passed by the railway, which had its own interchange with the River Severn. By this time it was reported that the 'inclines and engines are dropping together into ruin, almost unserviceable'. However, the Hay inclined plane continued to be used by the Madeley Wood Company for the transportation of coal and iron from Blists Hill until 1894, so had a life of over 100 years. The incline and the adjacent section of the canal were formally closed in 1907 when an agreement was made between the Madeley Wood Company and the LNWR.

Roads were never much of an alternative to river transport, and any potential they may have had was soon eclipsed by standard-gauge railways. In his description of Shropshire in 1803, Archdeacon Joseph Plymley wrote 'the roads in this county, both turnpike and private, are generally bad'. Private roads were said to be particularly poor: they were not attended to by their owners because the Highway Act was so easy to evade. Plymley put forward proposals for improvements, such as the appointment of surveyors by magistrates, the appointment of inspectors, and the installation of weigh-bridges at toll gates. Overloaded wagons were destroying the roads and one of the reasons cited was the high price of draught horses. The report exhorted local farmers to keep breeding mares. For the middle parishes of Shropshire, Plymley noted that 'there is no tolerable horse-road whatever, and in some that have coal and lime, those articles are nearly useless'. The coal- and ironmasters of Broseley, Coalbrookdale and Madeley, would only send their cargoes by road under pressure, for example when water levels in the Severn were so low that it was not navigable for months on end. In 1796, the river was only open for two months of the year. In 1803, conditions were so bad that Boulton and Watt of the Soho Foundry, near Birmingham, arranged for Shropshire iron to be sent by road.

The location of the Iron Bridge was partly influenced by the existing Madeley turnpike, which ran in a north-westerly direction towards Lincoln Hill (see **19-21, colour plate 4**). When the bridge was erected in 1779, new approach roads were required: a link road was made between the bridge and the Madeley turnpike, whilst a new road was started in 1779 which ran south from the bridge towards Benthall. A new turnpike between Ironbridge and Madeley, which became Madeley Road, was built in 1806-10 and required major engineering works to retain the hillside.

The state of roads improved after the end of the Napoleonic wars in 1815, when employment schemes were set up to relieve the poor in the ensuing depression. Some of these involved building roads under the supervision of local turnpike trusts. The present road up Jiggers Bank in Coalbrookdale was constructed, whilst other local roads were widened or improved.

On a different scale altogether was Thomas Telford's Holyhead Road. Passing through Priorslee, Ketley and Wellington to the north of the Ironbridge Gorge, the route was planned by the Government to link London with Dublin. Telford was commissioned to survey the road in England and Wales. Between 1815 and 1835, improvements were made to the sections which passed through the East Shropshire Coalfield including major engineering works such as the construction of by-passes and embankments. The new road was very useful to the local ironmasters, much improving the transportation of iron to Birmingham and the Black Country. However, freight traffic on the Holyhead Road underwent a massive decline with the coming of the railways.

Standard-gauge railways came to Shropshire relatively late, in the 1860s, long after the railway boom years of the 1830s and 1840s. Competition between the largest companies, such as the Great Western Railway (GWR) and London and North Western Railway (LNWR), was a spur to their development in the coalfield, to the extent that too many were constructed and they were not viable in the long term. Local industrialists were not slow to see their potential and backed proposals that were advantageous to them. Railways allowed heavy goods to be transported at speed to almost limitless destinations. This had a profound effect on River Severn traffic, which declined rapidly, and also on the associated industries. Thomas Griffiths of the Coalport Woodworks was a builder of boats and barges. When boat traffic declined, his business was no longer viable so he became a timber merchant. By 1851 there was only one barge builder left in the area, Edward Gother of Bower Yard (**31**). The trust which ran the horse-towing path along the river between Coalbrookdale and Bewdley wound up in 1885, whilst the last commercial boat to sail on the Severn in Shropshire was in 1895. Fatefully, the boat sank after hitting Bridgnorth Bridge.

Three main railways passed through the Ironbridge area, roughly forming a triangle. The London and North Western Railway (Coalport branch) ran from Wellington in a south-easterly direction towards Coalport East Station where it terminated. It was completed in 1861 and partly replaced the Shropshire Canal. Great Western Railway's Severn Junction branch also began in Wellington, running south to Lightmoor. The section through Coalbrookdale, including the Albert Edward Bridge over the Severn, was completed in 1864 (**33, 58**).

33 *Coalbrookdale station in the early twentieth century. The church is in the far distance*

The line that perhaps had the greatest significance was the Severn Valley Railway that followed the river from Shrewsbury, through Ironbridge and Bridgnorth, to Worcester. The SVR board was set up in 1852 but the railway did not open until 1862 because of financial problems and opposition from other railways companies and the owner of Apley Estate to the east of Coalport Bridge, who did not want his view ruined by steam trains. Tradesmen, however, were strongly supportive, stating that the cost of sending freight by river was 10 shillings per ton, whilst it was 7-8 shillings per ton by rail. The engineer was Robert Nicholson. Factories were subsequently built alongside the railway and new sidings were specially constructed for them. Good examples are the Craven Dunnill Tileworks and the Maws Tileworks in Jackfield.

7

THE CLAY INDUSTRIES: POTTERY AND PORCELAIN

In 1799 Coalport was described as 'the largest and most expensive porcelain producing estate in Great Britain'. Two neighbouring factories, bordering the River Severn and the Shropshire Canal, attracted tourists, industrial spies, engineers and even royalty: Local newspapers reported that the Prince and Princess of Orange went to Coalport in August 1796 and bought some pieces of John Rose's china. What is perhaps surprising is how quickly these factories developed — the visit took place only a year after their founding. The factories were the dominant enterprises of the Coalport new town. According to Thomas Telford in 1800, 250 people were employed in the porcelain factory and 150 in the pottery. This was indeed large, even in comparison with Staffordshire. So what were the factors which led to such success in the production of ceramics?

Pottery production was established in East Shropshire by the seventeenth century and was concentrated on the south bank of the River Severn in Jackfield and Benthall. Potters were attracted by the outcrops of suitable clay and coal, and frequently sited their potworks on these seams. Subsequently, it was found that clay mined from below-ground seams made a much better quality product. When factory-scale production developed from domestic production in the late eighteenth century, the proximity of the River Severn was another significant factor.

Documentary evidence for the pottery industry up to the late eighteenth century is surprisingly sparse. We know that there were close links between Jackfield and the Staffordshire Potteries, not only in terms of technology but also the potters themselves, who migrated from one area to the other. The true significance of the Jackfield pottery industry, especially in comparison with Staffordshire, is not fully understood and will remain an important area of archaeological research.

The earliest recorded pottery vessel at Jackfield was a brown earthenware mug dated 1634, discovered in an old coal pit, but unfortunately the mug no longer survives. A place by the River Severn called Salthouses has revealed sherds of white salt-glazed stoneware dated 1700–20, a very distinctive type compared to the earlier earthenwares and slipwares. Stoneware was made of clay and sand fired at such a high temperature that it vitrified. It had a hard, white, translucent body and a shiny hard glaze that was achieved by throwing salt through funnels in the roof of the kiln. Salthouses had previously been a centre for small-scale salt production which may explain this new direction. A subsequent development occurred in Staffordshire in 1725 when an earthenware body was produced — using white clays from south-west England and ground flint — which looked very similar to Chinese porcelain. It was known as creamware. A variety of new techniques ensued, and led to a major expansion in the pottery industry including trade to the British colonies.

Jackfield became well-known for its shiny black-glazed jugs and decanters, known as Jackfield Ware. The black glaze was applied to a red earthenware body and sometimes had coloured or gilded flowers and scrolls in relief. The last pottery-type made in Jackfield before production changed to decorative tiles was mocha-ware. This is an earthenware with a distinctive feather-like pattern in yellow and brown, created by dropping a liquid containing tobacco juice on to the slip before it had a chance to dry.

Nineteenth-century historians of the Jackfield pottery industry, who used sources no longer available, suggested that the Thursfield family, who had a long tenure in the area, dominated the trade. John Thursfield I (1707–60) came from Staffordshire to work in the pottery of Joseph Garner around 1723. He is said to have made salt-glazed stonewares. By 1773–4 there were at least three potworks in Jackfield (see **5**): Morris Thursfield (son of John Thursfield) had a potworks on what is now the site of the Jackfield Tile Museum, known as the Jackfield Pottery. The other potteries were owned by Richard Simpson and Thursfield & Bell (John Thursfield II). It was Morris Thursfield who was held responsible for manufacturing the highly successful Jackfield Ware and marketing it across the Atlantic. He apparently died in Philadelphia whilst selling his products there in 1783. The Jackfield Pottery was subsequently taken over by Edward Blakeway, a businessman and industrialist of Broseley Hall, who was joined by John Rose, a young apprentice from Caughley, where they are said to have embarked on the manufacture of porcelain (**34**). This has been confirmed by porcelain sherds excavated at the site. After Blakeway and Rose had moved to Coalport in 1795–6, ceramic production continued in Jackfield, but reverting back to earthenware. The factory was taken over a number of times and was known variously as the Ash Tree Potworks (see **2**), the Ivanhoe Pottery, and the Wootton and Jackfield Pottery. It was converted to an encaustic tileworks in 1867.

Several potteries are known in Benthall and neighbouring Posenhall, again located on seams of coal and clay. Salt-glazed stonewares of 1700–20, along with lead-glazed earthenwares and slipwares were found on the site of the later vicarage in Benthall. John Thursfield II set up a pottery around 1743 on land belonging to the Willey estate, which was known as the Haybrook Pottery, or Mughouse, because of the number of drinking mugs that it produced for local public houses. They were mainly of yellow or brown earthenware with white slip decoration. Thursfield was succeeded by his son, also John, and they started another pottery on the other side of the road, which became known as the Benthall Pottery. A further works in Benthall was the Pitchyard Pottery at Spout Lane, thought to have begun in the eighteenth century and where slipware sherds were found in the 1950s. It may have been run by William Lloyd of Pitchyard House and his widow, from before 1814 until at least 1833. The site subsequently became a factory for making clay tobacco pipes.

A major advance occurred in 1775 with the establishment of the first porcelain factory in Shropshire. This time the connections were with Worcester rather than with Staffordshire, so porcelain production did not occur as a natural progression from earthenware production. The factory was at Caughley, on top of a hill about a mile

34 *John Rose (1771–1841) was the leading figure in the development of porcelain in Shropshire. He founded the Coalport Chinaworks with his business partner, Edward Blakeway, and made a number of innovations such as lead-free glazes*

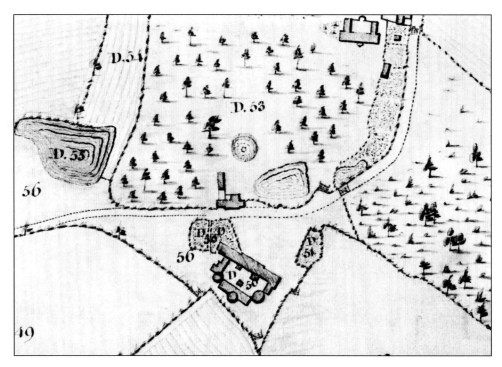

35 *The Caughley Chinaworks was erected in 1772, in an isolated position close to supplies of coal and clay. It was unable to compete with the Coalport Chinaworks and after the amalgamation of the two factories it quickly declined. The factory closed around 1815 and the workers were moved to Coalport. The courtyard plan is typical of a potworks of this period*

south of the river and not far from Broseley. In 1866, the art-historian Llewellynn Jewitt described the Caughley Chinaworks as 'perfectly retired from the world, situated in the midst of woods and wilds, almost unapproachable to strangers, and with every facility for keeping the workmen away from all chance of imparting secrets to others' (**35**). Espionage was a real issue through the eighteenth and nineteenth centuries and also had an effect on the layout of potworks buildings. The main reason for the isolated location of the factory, however, was the abundant supply of coal less than 20ft (6.1m) below the ground, along with seams of 'clunch', the fire-clay that was so suitable for making pottery and saggars.

There was an earlier pottery at Caughley, started by Mr Browne of Caughley Hall — apparently in 1751 — which was taken over by his relative, Mr Gallimore, who renewed a lease in 1754 for a term of 62 years. Nothing is known of the earthenware vessels that were produced there. Mr Gallimore was replaced as proprietor in 1772 by his son-in-law, Thomas Turner of Worcester, who began to trade as the Salopian Porcelain Manufactory. The factory was rebuilt a few hundred metres to the north and is said to have incorporated a foundation stone near the entrance bearing the date 1772. A local newspaper reported that the factory was complete by 1775 and was producing vessels which 'in colour and fineness are truly elegant and beautiful, and have the bright and lively white of the so much extolled Oriental'. By this time, clay for the porcelain bodies would have come from Devon and Cornwall.

Because Worcester did not have the benefit of local coal deposits, some undecorated wares were transported from Caughley to Chamberlain's of Worcester for finishing. However, some vessels also went the other way: this time from Grainger & Co of Worcester to Caughley for printing, before being returned to Worcester. Caughley had by this time developed a reputation for its under-glaze printing techniques. The early examples of Caughley were close to earthenware, but the fabric became finer and more translucent as a result of significant developments in technology. Thomas Turner was said to be a keen chemist as well as an excellent draughtsman and introduced willow pattern and the blue dragon pattern into England. The shape of the vessels was also unusual and apparently difficult to attain. Turner was not averse to espionage himself, and around 1780 he travelled to Sèvres in France where he gained new knowledge about porcelain manufacture, and brought some skilled workers back with him.

The blue-and-white Oriental-style patterns introduced by Turner were applied by under-glaze printing (**colour plate 9**): The designs were engraved on copper plates, whilst the colours were prepared on a stove and suspended in hot oil. The colour was spread over the surface of the plate, which was then cleaned so that the colour was only in the interstices. An impression was made on thin tissue paper using a hand operated roller, which was then applied to the vessel. It was rubbed briskly and the vessel thrown into a vat of hot water so that the paper peeled off leaving the pattern behind (**36**).

The Caughley porcelain factory had a courtyard plan much like Worcester and many of the Staffordshire potteries (see **35**). Such a layout was helpful in making the factory safe from prying eyes, but in addition each workroom could be entered by a door or stairs directly from the courtyard so that the workers would know only the secrets of their own trade. The vessels were frequently carried between workrooms by children. Some of the workmen lived at the factory, which employed about 100 people, while Thomas Turner is said to have had a French 'chateau' built close to the works by one of the craftsmen he had brought back from France. The earlier pottery at Caughley was converted for saggar-making. The word 'saggar' derives from 'safeguard' and they were basically round earthenware tubs with straight sides that were stacked on top of each other in the kiln to protect the ware. It was quite unusual for a factory to have a separate saggar works — normally the saggars were made on site by the workmen at the glazing kiln.

Thomas Turner's Caughley works was a great success until the 1790s, when he met with competition from John Rose and partners at Coalport (see **34**). In 1798–9 he was forced out of business. John Rose took over the factory but found it uneconomical: the easily available coal on the site had been mainly worked out and its distance from the river attracted additional costs. Women carried the finished ware the whole distance from Caughley to Coalport (ironic given that the area was known for its early wooden railways). The workforce at Caughley, many of whom were highly skilled, was slowly moved to Coalport. This operation was complete by about 1815, but the buildings were not allowed to go to waste either. By 1821 they had all been taken down, including Thomas Turner's house, and the bricks were transported to Coalport where they were used for enlarging the factory and building workmen's houses. By the mid-nineteenth century there was

36 *In this engraving showing transfer printing, the colours are prepared on the stove in the background, and are then rubbed into an engraved design on a copper plate. A thin sheet of tissue paper is rolled over the copper plate, to pick up the design, and is then briskly applied to the vessel*

nothing to see of Caughley. Anything surviving below ground was destroyed in the 1960s during open-casting, except for the site of the saggar-making works which is still extant. All that we have left from the china factory are the vessels themselves and a few sherds.

The history of pottery and porcelain production on the north side of the River Severn is quite different. The huge factories at Coalport were established quickly as part of the new town, which followed the construction of the Shropshire Canal in 1790–3. John Rose, his brother Richard, and Edward Blakeway set up the Coalport porcelain factory in a pottery said to have belonged to a Mr Young, a mercer of Shrewsbury. No evidence for this pottery has ever been found, but if it existed, it must have been short-lived because in 1788 the area was nothing but fields and meadows. The factory was started in 1795 and completed in 1796, when Charles Hatchett noted in his diary 'a Porcelain Manufactory lately established. The ware is like that of Worcester and the materials the same'.

Rose and Blakeway had absorbed the Caughley Chinaworks by 1799, but they appear to have had trouble recruiting skilled staff for gilding, enamelling and blue painting, as

37 *Women painters at the Coalport Chinaworks, photographed in the early twentieth century. This was skilled work, although women were barred from the highest status jobs. The building they are working in is now a youth hostel*

revealed by a stream of adverts in the local Shropshire newspapers. This situation was exacerbated in the Autumn of 1799 as a result of a fatal accident. It was reported in the *Shrewsbury Chronicle* that a ferry transporting 43 workers to their homes on the south bank of the Severn had capsized, resulting in 28 deaths.

China decorators were skilled and sought after, some gaining a national reputation and moving around between different establishments. Sometimes they signed their work, and their designs can be found in the Coalport pattern-books. John Randall, born in Broseley in 1810, was a bird painter, and worked in the Rockingham factory and at his uncle Thomas Martin Randall's works in Madeley, as well as at Coalport. Painting was also undertaken by women, and was regarded as a high status job (**37**). Enamelling was done by laying oil on the relevant parts of the vessel and then adding colours with cotton wool. This was known as ground laying. The enamel colours had to be fixed by firing in an enamelling kiln.

John Rose, Edward Blakeway and Robert Winter (who had replaced Richard Rose in 1799) were declared bankrupt in 1803. The Coalport and Caughley china factories were bought by Cuthbert Johnson and William Clark, but with John Rose continuing as manager. Subsequently, the company was known as John Rose & Co.

John Rose's china factory was situated between the Shropshire Canal and the High Street, but a second factory was started on the opposite side of the canal at about the same time. The early years of this factory remain elusive, but Joshua Gilpin, an American industrialist and merchant, visited in 1796 and noted 'Mr. Reynolds' Pottery lately established here — makes the yellow ware as good and cheap as Staffordshire, also China very good'. The ferry accident in 1799 included pottery workers amongst the victims. The pottery continued in 1800 under a new partnership that was established between William Reynolds, William Horton and Thomas Rose. The latter was the younger brother of John Rose and had been apprenticed to his rival, Thomas Turner, at Caughley. Thomas Telford visited a few months after the establishment of the partnership and noted that they made earthenware in imitation of that made at Etruria and called the Queen's or Wedgwood ware. Porcelain was also being manufactured which was distinguishable from John Rose's china. William Reynolds died in 1803 and his share in the partnership was taken by his cousin, Robert Anstice.

Another problem in the early history of Coalport is the pottery of Walter Bradley & Co. Bradley was a business associate of William Reynolds and was also referred to as an accountant. The earliest known possible piece of Bradley's ware is a creamware commemoration mug with an inscription 'Manufactured at Coalport 1797'. As well as creamware, he made black basalt ware and red caneware (**colour plate 10**). Bradley was also a merchandiser and opened a 'Wholesale Earthenware Warehouse' at the Canal Wharf in Shrewsbury in 1797. It seems logical that he might have been an agent at William Reynolds' pottery, but the significant drawback to this theory is that no sherds of Bradley's ware have ever been excavated at the Coalport Chinaworks, so the pottery may have been made elsewhere.

A pottery is shown next to Swinney Mill, downstream of Coalport Bridge, in several paintings (**38**). It only has one kiln, suggesting that coarse earthenwares were being produced for the local domestic market rather than anything more refined. A manufacturer of porcelain or refined earthenwares would normally need at least two kilns, one for the initial biscuit firing, and another for the glaze firing. The glazing kiln was normally smaller than the biscuit kiln and was fired at a lower but more critical temperature. The owner of the Swinney pottery remains a mystery but it is unlikely to have been Walter Bradley.

The layout of the Coalport factories originally consisted of linear ranges with hovel kilns at their ends, following the lines of the Shropshire Canal, the River Severn and the High Street. This was quite different from the more common courtyard plans found at Caughley, Worcester and in Staffordshire. However, secrecy could still have been maintained and it is likely that the upper-storey workshops were reached by their own external staircases. The best evidence for the appearance of the factories is a painting on a vase, the reverse side of which is signed by Thomas Baxter, a London decorator (**colour plate 11**). It is likely to date to around 1810–14, by which time the factories had grown from their original size.

One of the buildings shown in this depiction was the flint mill owned by Anstice, Horton and Rose on the south side of the canal. It was also described by an engineer, Simon Goodrich, in 1803: 'Saw the mills grinding the flint and . . . there were 4 pans one large one on the ground floor and 3 smaller in a room above driven by a single power

38 *Swinney Mill, downstream from Coalport Bridge, is shown in a number of early nineteenth-century views with an adjacent pottery kiln. The pottery is otherwise unknown, but probably had a short life*

atmospherical steam engine'. Preparation of raw materials — clay, flint, bone and colours — was the first step in the manufacturing process. Flint had to be calcined in a kiln to make it whiter and more brittle before it was ground in large circular pans with revolving wooden paddles and chert runners. Early mills tended to be water powered, but many of the later ones, as at Coalport, were powered by steam. The flint was ground to a thick paste and was then mixed with a fine suspension of clay, resulting in a compound called slip. This was dried in a slip-kiln, a trough that was heated underneath, and when it had attained the consistency of dough it was taken out and stored in damp cellars for several months where it fermented and disintegrated. Slip-kilns became less common during the nineteenth century, and a filter and press were normally used to get rid of excess water instead.

The partnership of Anstice, Horton and Rose was dissolved in 1814 and the factory was taken over by John Rose & Co who combined the two works. By this time earthenware production had ceased. The amalgamation, along with the integration of the Caughley workforce, must have led to a significant reorganisation of work. This process continued after 1820 when the Swansea porcelain works was closed and the moulds and workmen were moved to Coalport. In the same year the Nantgarw works near Cardiff was bought out by John Rose & Co. By 1837, the Coalport Chinaworks was recorded by Charles Hulbert as 'giving employment to 800 hands'. This period not only saw expansion but significant technical developments. In 1820, John Rose was awarded a gold medal by the Society of Arts for inventing a lead-free glaze. The glaze was achieved by adding felspar, and John Rose advertised his ware accordingly as 'Coalport Felspar Porcelain'. Before

John Rose's invention, dipping the vessels into the glaze solution after their first firing was the most dangerous occupation in a pottery. The active ingredients were white lead and sometimes arsenic, and the dipper frequently suffered paralysis, epilepsy and digestive problems, sometimes leading to death.

Of all the types of vessels produced, tea and coffee wares were the most common, particularly tea bowls, cups and saucers. Also found are teapots, sugar bowls and milk or cream jugs. Table wares included round and oval plates, with a range of decorations to the rims, whilst less common items were meat drainers, teapot stands and trays. Jugs and vases of a purely ornamental nature were also made, some commissioned especially to commemorate events such as elections (**colour plate 12**). Styles in the early nineteenth century still focussed on blue-printed and oriental designs, whilst a development around 1820 was the revival of the Rococo style, with relief-moulded floral designs becoming increasingly popular. The 'Coalbrookdale' style, which evolved in the 1820s out of German forms, was well known for its flower-encrusted vases of a purely ornamental nature (**colour plate 13**). After the 1840s decoration in the Sèvres style became fashionable, with particular emphasis on colours — notably ground colours and bird painting.

The techniques employed for making vessels of different forms were throwing, moulding or pressing. Flat vessels such as plates and dishes would be either cast or pressed into plaster moulds. Rounded vessels such as cups or jugs were thrown using a hand-operated wheel. Afterwards, they would go to the turner to be smoothed and regulated, and then on to the handler who would attach the handles, spouts, and ornamentation to the bodies. All the vessels would be taken to the stove-house to be dried, before being placed in saggars in the biscuit kiln for the first firing.

After the biscuit firing was the glazing. When the dipped vessels were ready to be placed in the glazing kiln, they were put into saggars on a layer of coarsely ground flint. After being removed from the kiln, the pots had to be scoured to remove the flint that had stuck to them. The air in the scouring room became charged with particles of dust that lined the lungs and led to consumption and cancer. Other workshops containing dust were equally dangerous — the ground layers in the enamelling shops were likely to inhale colour dust, normally a mixture of metallic oxides. The children who carried the vessels between workshops were at risk of serious illness because they had to endure significant changes in temperature.

John Rose died in 1841 and his place was taken by his younger brother, Thomas Rose, until he died two years later. A period of decline ensued, and a receiver was appointed in 1875 to sort out years of poor management including excessive stock-piling. Five years later, in 1880, the chinaworks was sold for £15,000 to Peter Schuyler Bruff, an East Anglian engineer. In the same year, the works was described by local historian and former employee John Randall. It was:

> ill designed and badly constructed, the greater portion of them having been put up at the latter end of the past and beginning of the present centuries . . . with no regard to ventilation or other requirements of health. Consequently there are the most curious ins and outs, dropsical looking roofs, bulging walls and drooping floors, which have been propped underneath . . . In entering some of

39 *Coalport in the early twentieth century, viewed across a timber yard and showing the scale of kilns and workshops. Of the three kilns in the foreground, the central one is by far the oldest, and had been constructed by 1803. It partially survives today*

these unhealthy *ateliers* . . . strangers have to look well to their craniums. Some work-rooms have very stifling atmospheres, charged with clay or flint; the biscuit room notably so.

Peter Bruff's son Charles was appointed managing director in 1888 and devoted himself to restoring the factory to its former glories. His determination was rewarded and major changes ensued, beginning with the appointment of a new art director, Thomas John Bott, and the installation of central heating. In the first decade of the twentieth century many of the buildings were taken down and new ones erected in their place, representing a considerable investment (**39**). John Randall described the Coalport Chinaworks for a second time in 1908: 'Considerable improvements have been effected both in the approach to the works, which has been planted with trees, and in the exterior and interior of the buildings themselves, which are better lighted and better ventilated. Under the new Factory Act . . . quite a revolution has taken place . . . to protect the operatives from the injurious effects of the deleterious matter necessarily employed . . . in colours, and from the dust arising from grinding and dressing.'

The only other porcelain factory on the north side of the River Severn was Thomas Martin Randall's Chinaworks at Madeley. He had been an apprentice at Caughley under John Rose, and then went to Derby and London. He came back to Madeley and set up a works in 1826 in the lower part of the town. Some difficulties ensued with firing because he was a decorator rather than a manufacturer, but this was soon overcome and china in the Sèvres style was made. He employed some of the best decorators, such as Enos Raby, a ground layer and gilder, and William Cook who painted flowers. Both these men subsequently worked at the Coalport Chinaworks. Randall's establishment closed when he moved to Shelton in the Potteries where he was offered a partnership by Herbert Minton, but he retired soon afterwards.

Contemporary with decorative tiles in the late nineteenth century was 'Art Pottery', which was influenced by Art Nouveau and Classical styles. This was mainly made on the south side of the river, the Benthall Pottery under William Allen being the main producer. It was a short-lived fashion, however, and by the turn of the century the Benthall Pottery was mainly producing coarse wares. By the early twentieth century, the Shropshire pottery and porcelain industries were struggling to compete with Staffordshire. The last manufacturer was Coalport, but after some years running at a loss the factory was sold in 1924 to Cauldon Potteries of Staffordshire. In 1926 the Coalport Chinaworks was closed and the employees were moved to Shelton.

8
THE CLAY INDUSTRIES: BRICKS, TILES AND TOBACCO PIPES

The mechanisation and mass-production of bricks was a relatively late phenomenon, taking place from the mid-nineteenth century, not only in Shropshire, but across the whole country. The Victorian building boom and the coming of the railways were important factors leading to the expansion. A similar pattern occurred with the production of decorative tiles, for much the same reasons. The East Shropshire Coalfield was an ideal location for making bricks and tiles because of the suitable clays and coal. In fact these products were made from an early date but only on a small scale. Another important clay industry was the manufacture of tobacco pipes. This was a more specialised and localised activity centred on the town of Broseley.

Bricks were made in the district from at least the seventeenth century, and are to be found in such prestige buildings as Willey Hall, of 1618. By the eighteenth century brick was the most common building material, and the growth caused by industrialisation is manifested by the many brick buildings that can still be seen today. There are historical references to some of the brickworks but little physical evidence. For example, William Reynolds had brickworks at the Lloyds and at Coalport, but their locations are uncertain. The Coalport brickworks that made bricks for the Coalport 'new town' may have been south east of the Chinaworks.

The reason why the seventeenth- and eighteenth-century brick-making industry has left no trace is the ephemeral nature of production. Clay winning or getting was generally a surface operation. The clay would be weathered for long periods and might be washed and mixed by stamping it in pits. Occasionally it was mixed in a pug mill, an upright wooden cylinder containing blades, which was operated by a horse walking round in circles in much the same way as a horse gin. The bricks were formed by hand, dried in stacks, and then fired in small updraught kilns or temporary clamps (**40**).

This method of production continued well into the nineteenth century. However, in Broseley, there was a change from the later eighteenth century that had important repercussions. Clay getting became an offshoot of the mining industry, so was brought from shafts and adits. Clay layers are interspersed with coal in the Upper and Middle Coal Measures, the latter alone containing about 90 different strata. Many of the clay layers have different properties and were suited to particular products. This led to the diversification and specialisation of the clay industries, especially on the south bank of the River Severn in Broseley and Jackfield, which became famous for roof tiles, white bricks,

40 *Until mechanisation in the second half of the nineteenth century, bricks were hand-made in temporary buildings, often by women. On the right of the picture is a small pug mill, its paddles turned by a horse. Behind is the kiln. Little archaeological evidence of such works has ever been found*

common bricks and specials, not to mention decorative tiles, pottery and clay tobacco pipes. Mines were soon sunk specifically to get clay.

There was an enormous expansion of the industry in the nineteenth century. Only two large works are known in 1750, Hollygrove Tileries in Jackfield and the Horsehay Brickworks north of Coalbrookdale, both of which had a long history. By 1850 there were at least 18 brick and tile works in the district, and in 1900 the number had grown to over 30.

Whilst specialist materials were being produced on the south side of the river and transported large distances, first by river and then by railway, the situation to the north was slightly different. Some of the brickworks were owned and operated by the Coalbrookdale Company or the Madeley Wood Company, whose main concerns were coal and iron. It was profitable to get clay from shafts after the coal and ironstone seams had been exhausted. As well as selling the bricks, the companies used them at their own works. Examples are the brick and tile works at Blists Hill, owned by the Madeley Wood Company, and the Coalbrookdale Company's Lightmoor Brickworks.

Mechanisation from the 1870s led to the construction of planned, integrated brick and tile-making factories. They were steam driven, the power being transmitted by means of line shafts and belt drives, to clay preparation, extrusion and cutting machines. Gravity also played its part as it was normal for the raw materials to be loaded onto the top floor of the works, and to emerge as unfired bricks from the bottom, from where they were taken to the drying sheds and kilns.

41 *Compound clay preparation machines, utilising gravity, were universally used in the late nineteenth-century brick trade. The clay was passed through kibblers and rollers, and then its plasticity was improved by passing it through screw mechanisms known as pug mills. Finally the clay was extruded into a continuous stream and formed into bricks by wire cutters on a bench at the bottom. Power was provided by steam engines and transmitted by means of belt drives*

There were, however, some important inventions earlier in the nineteenth century, most of which were dependent on the successful use of cast iron. Relevant to the brick industry, and particularly the manufacture of decorative tiles, was Richard Prosser's semi-dry process for making ceramic buttons, patented in 1840. Clay dust was compacted in an iron press, reducing the amount of time and fuel required to dry the product. Presses capable of producing smooth facing bricks were introduced during the 1870s, whilst the first wire-cutting machine was designed by Richard Bennett in 1879. Compound brick-making machines were available by the end of the nineteenth century where the milled clay was fed into one end, and came out of the other end as a continuous stream ready for wire-cutting (**41**). There had been refinements in the semi-dry process of brick manufacture by this time: at the Donnington Wood Brickworks, further north in Telford, unweathered clay was taken straight into the works and ground to a fine powder in a circular pan. A contemporary development was the semi-plastic method of manufacture where the milled clay was mixed with a little water in a large, circular pan, then went through several crushing and mixing stages before reaching the extrusion machine, by which time it was very stiff. Like the semi-dry process, the semi-plastic process led to increased efficiency and output.

Improvements also occurred in kiln technology, allowing the flow of air to be varied so that different colours and finishes could be produced. The brick and tile works on both sides of the River Severn mainly had intermittent downdraught kilns, which were ideally suited to relatively small works where considerable control over firing could be achieved. A downdraught kiln had a separate chimney, the two being linked by a flue. Heat from the fireboxes passed round the kiln evenly before being drawn up the chimney. In an updraught kiln, the heat passed straight out of the top. Continuous rather than intermittently-fired kilns were only needed in large brickworks. The first was designed by Friedrich Hoffman of Berlin in 1858 and patented in Britain by Humphrey Chamberlain, followed by numerous modifications. It was only in the north part of the East Shropshire Coalfield, such as at Donnington Wood, that such kilns were constructed.

A series of Public Health Acts from the late nineteenth century, ordering piped clean water and a comprehensive sewage system, led to an enormous demand for glazed ceramic pipes which continued until the mid-twentieth century. This had far reaching social consequences, particularly for health and in the daily lives of women. Production in some existing brick and tile works was changed over to pipes, such as the Bower Yard white brickworks in the 1920s. The Horsehay Brickworks at Pool Hill was first recorded in 1733 when it was producing firebricks, along with common bricks and tiles. In 1900 it became the Days Sanitary Pipe Company.

Hollygrove Tileries in Jackfield is particularly interesting because it spanned most of the major changes in brick and tile manufacture. The Beard family were producing tiles here in 1584 and continued to do so for many generations. In 1815 the works was owned by Samuel Roden, also a tobacco pipe manufacturer. There were subsequent changes of ownership until 1867 when it was purchased by John Bennett Lawes of Middlesex. The land itself was owned by Lord Forester and a lease records not only the brick and tile yard, but the clay mine and wharves on the River Severn. A list of the goods manufactured includes common bricks and tiles, specials (such as crest tiles and brewhouse floor bricks), and a large range of drainage pipes, mainly for agricultural use. In the 1870s the works was taken over by John Wilkinson, a local farmer. He appears to have rebuilt the works to a significant degree, so that by the time he leased it to Richard Haughton in 1884 it had two engines, a brick machine, tile presses, two drying sheds and five kilns. Wilkinson had decided on specialisation, patenting interlocking tiles and producing a variety of decorative specials such as finials. The works probably closed down during the 1914–18 war, by which time it was also making glazed sanitary pipes. Unfortunately, nothing survives of the factory buildings.

The Blists Hill Brick & Tile Works, on the east and west sides of the Shropshire Canal, is by far the best preserved example in the district. It was built in the 1870s by the Madeley Wood Company, but there was an earlier brickworks on the site, present by 1847, where hand-made bricks were fired in a simple kiln. The new works was specially designed to house a steam engine, so mechanisation must have been planned. By 1902 the factory had grown and bricks were being made by the semi-plastic process. It was acquired by George Legge & Sons in 1912 (and purchased outright from the Madeley Wood Company in 1916), but went into liquidation in 1938. During this period, hand-made bricks and tiles became a speciality, produced using different clays and varying the amount of air that passed through the kilns. One of the kiln firemen recorded that the products ranged from blue through brindled to a very red strawberry colour. Sanitary pipes were made between 1945 and 1956. The end of brick and tile production in about 1940 was common in the Ironbridge Gorge. By this time the massive brickworks focused on the London clays, around Peterborough, Bedfordshire and the Medway Valley, had a firm grip on the national market. The only remaining brick manufacturer in East Shropshire is Blockleys in north Telford.

There were three major producers of decorative tiles in Victorian Britain which not only found their way to all corners of the nation but effectively conquered the English-speaking world. Railways allowed such weighty items to be transported to a wide range of destinations much more easily. The Victorian building boom was far-reaching: growth in house building and the development of suburbs; public houses, theartres and hotels; great municipal buildings such as town halls and hospitals. A great wave of church building and restoration occurred, mostly in the Gothic-Revival style. The Public Health Acts led to a requirement for glazed products, not only pipes but facing tiles, for example in food shops and railway stations.

The first of the major decorative tile companies was Minton Hollins of Stoke-on-Trent, followed by Maw of Benthall (and later Jackfield) and Craven Dunnill of Jackfield. Minton Hollins and the two Jackfield factories were designed by the same architect, Charles Lynam of Stoke-on-Trent. Whilst the tiles of Minton and Maws are perhaps the most well-known, Craven Dunnill is of special interest because of the complete preservation of its factory.

Herbert Minton had an association with Shropshire as his father was an engraver at the Caughley Chinaworks. He attempted to imitate medieval encaustic tiles in 1828, but the patent went to Samuel Wright of Shelton, Staffordshire, who in the end partly disposed of his patent to Minton, and to George Barr of Worcester. Encaustic tiles had impressions into which a different coloured clay was inlaid. The second colour could be due to a different type of clay, or was made by adding a metallic oxide. In the late 1830s red, buff or chocolate were the only colours available. These tiles were made in moulds using the 'plastic' process, as they had been since medieval times.

It was Herbert Minton who saw the potential of Prosser's semi-dry process for making buttons, and he subsequently bought into the patent. By 1842 Minton had 60 tile presses, in which the dry clay dust was crushed between two metal dies. As for bricks and common tiles, this led to much more efficient use of fuel and time. For encaustic tiles the semi-dry process was only perfected after 1863, when the inlay dust was put into the bottom die and the rest of the clay added afterwards.

The preparation of clay for tile manufacture was undertaken in much the same way as for bricks. Surface clays were often dug, and were left to weather in heaps for a considerable time before going into the works. A. C. Fox-Davies, a visitor to Craven Dunnill in 1890, reported that the 'clay undergoes a very severe operation, and it leaves the grinding mills in a fluid state'. It was then passed through silk sieves into tanks, from where it was pumped into a drying kiln to remove the water. The clay was ground again in another mill, until it was 'as soft to the touch as flour'. The tiles were actually made in the pressing room where the cast iron dies exerted a pressure of about one ton per square inch. It was easy to produce tiles with relief decoration by using moulded dies, whilst colour effects could be made by simply varying the amount of glaze in the upper and lower surfaces. There were a variety of other finishes including under-glaze printing and painting and over-glaze enamelling. Printed tiles were made from copper plates and transfer paper in much the same way as porcelain (see **36**), whilst tiles could be hand-painted in coloured earth which would 'all come bright in the burning'.

The composition of glazes was a subject of much invention in the latter half of the nineteenth century. Opaque enamelling, known as majolica, was first brought in by Minton around 1850, but there was a great expansion in its use after 1875. The different coloured enamels were brushed or painted on, quite often onto relief moulding. It was a particularly popular technique with Craven Dunnill, whilst Maw & Co began to apply non-reflective glazes and enamels to their tiles. The expansion of decorative tiles as an applied art-form had an effect on other industries: for example, the Coalbrookdale Company began to make cast iron fireplaces with 'slip-out tile frames' so that tiles of the latest fashion could be inserted (**42**).

The history of the Maw family is particularly interesting as they came to the industry from an artistic background. The company was formed by John Hornby Maw and his sons, George and Arthur, but the whole family was involved in the enterprise. J. H. Maw was a farmer and chemist, but withdrew from business to pursue his artistic interests. The family moved round the country, from London to Hastings, then Devon, and finally Worcester. Maw had become interested in china clays in Devon and had many friends there who were potters. He was attracted by an advert for the Worcester Encaustic Tile Works, an offshoot of the Worcester Porcelain Company, and purchased it around 1850. Despite technical difficulties the family succeeded, but they were attracted to Broseley by its clays. In 1852 the Maw family and the whole of their workforce moved to Shropshire and set up the Benthall works. The tile designs were wide-ranging, to satisfy a diverse market, but many were their own creations (**colour plate 14**). George Maw was a keen botanist (with a speciality in the genus *crocus*) and plants were a common theme of the company's designs. He was also interested in archaeology and a series of tiles were made in the style of Roman mosaics (mosaics were normally made by women because of their smaller and more dextrous fingers) (**43**). Meanwhile his sister, Ann Mary, travelled the country copying tiles, particularly ecclesiastical examples, due to the popularity of the Gothic style and the vogue for church restoration. Members of the family also made occasional expeditions to Europe.

The company moved again in 1883, but this time only a short distance to Jackfield. The factory, designed by Charles Lynam, covered 4.8 acres (2ha) and was the largest decorative tileworks in the world. The company's catalogues were produced using the new process of colour lithography, not only displaying wall and floor tiles but recommending layouts and decorative schemes as well as arrangements for fireplaces (see **42, colour plate 15**).

Also in Jackfield was the factory of Craven Dunnill, started in 1871 (**44**). It was on the same principle of linear production, so that raw materials went into the factory at one end, passed through the departments, and emerged at the other end as the finished product. Both factories fronted the Severn Valley Railway that had been opened in 1862.

42 *Decorative tiles were commonly employed in fireplaces. This example is taken from the Maw & Co. catalogue. Note the 'Art Pottery' on the mantelpiece*

43 *Decorative tile-making was labour intensive. Here, women work in the mosaic workshop at the Craven Dunnill Tileworks. The vice-like fixtures on the benches are mosaic cutters*

The new tileworks was on the site of the Ash Tree Potworks (formerly the Jackfield Pottery) (see **2**). In 1867, it was converted to an encaustic tile works by its new owners, Hargreaves & Craven, who had moved from Broseley. They must have occupied the existing pottery buildings because a director of the company, J. P. G. Smith, reminisced that 'the place in which they commenced business looked broken down and the roof was falling', whilst a local newspaper reported in 1871, on the eve of its replacement, that the factory was 'decidedly the oldest in the neighbourhood'.

Henry Powell Dunnill (1821–95) was the key figure in the history of Craven Dunnill, becoming a shareholder and resident manager of the company in 1870. Born in Wakefield, and with no background in the clay industries, he was brought to Shropshire through his life-long passion for Liberalism when he went to stay with Alexander Hargreaves Brown, who was to become Liberal MP for Wenlock. Brown was a director of Hargreaves & Craven and, soon afterwards, Dunnill was asked to join the company. He was not at all impressed by his new surroundings and described Jackfield as 'not all the world but a very poor fag end of it . . . made up of pit-shafts, pit-mounds, rubbish heaps, brick ends, broken drain and roof and paving tiles, dilapidated houses . . . a neglected and forlorn place'. Despite his dislike of the place, Dunnill was a philanthropist and did much to encourage education and well-being amongst the people. For a few years he ran a profit-sharing scheme at the factory, and also started a savings bank although it attracted little interest. Later, he was instrumental in setting up Workmen's clubs in Jackfield and Broseley and providing them with books.

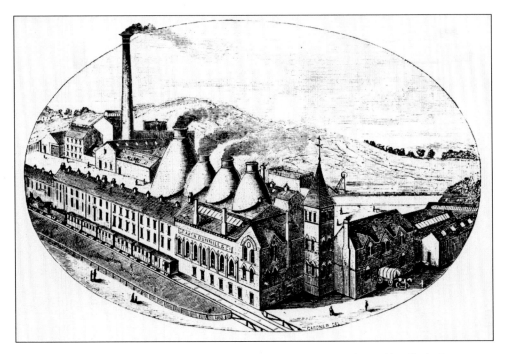

44 *The Craven Dunnill Decorative Tile Works was built in 1871 and was designed by Charles Lynam. This bird's eye view was used by the company in adverts. The railway influenced the location of the works, which was designed so that the preliminary processes were undertaken towards the rear, with the showroom and offices at the front. The kilns include biscuit kilns for firing the clay and a large glaze kiln*

The decision to build a new factory was made in 1870 on the founding of the new company of Hargreaves, Craven & Dunnill. Only a month later, two men were killed by a drying rack falling on top of them as a result of a wall collapsing, clearly showing the poor state of the old buildings. Following the designs of Charles Lynam, the new factory was begun in 1871 by William Exley, builders of Broseley. It was finally opened in 1874 (**44**). Subsequent changes were relatively minor, applying mainly to the kilns. As in the brick industry, most of the kilns had personal names: Fox-Davies saw the door of 'Miss Juno' being bricked up in 1890. In 1913, when the works was advertised for sale, it had three biscuit kilns and two glazing kilns. A Dressler kiln — a type of continuous kiln where the tiles were passed through on trucks — was installed in 1930 at the rear of the works. Production ceased during World War II.

It was not unknown for factories to produce both common and decorative tiles, and this was the case at the Broseley Tileries which had been started in 1760. By 1870 it was producing encaustic and glazed tiles for a variety of public buildings, including the Home and Colonial Offices, the Royal Academy, and the Law Offices at Lincoln's Inn, whilst common bricks and roofing tiles were still an important part of its repertoire (**colour plate 16**).

A clay industry special to Broseley was that of tobacco pipe manufacture. Smoking became fashionable in London in the sixteenth century, and by 1630 pipe manufacture had begun in Broseley based upon the suitable clays. In the eighteenth century, Broseley Wood and Benthall was one of the leading centres in Britain. There were families of pipe makers who thrived for generations, like the Leggs and the Rodens. The main market was in the Midlands, though some fragments have been found in the American Colonies. Broseley was especially known for its long-stemmed pipes that became known as 'Churchwardens', and these were closely connected with the Roden family. It was Noah Roden I who was the first to supply London clubs. By this time, clays from Devon had replaced the local clays, and it apparently acted as ballast in boats which had delivered coal to the Bristol ports. Production greatly increased throughout the eighteenth century although designs were generally conservative, some pipes having the maker's mark on the stem. In the early nineteenth century the many small domestic workshops were replaced by factories and the pipes were exported to a world-wide market. The industry was dominated by three firms who had many interconnections: William Southorn & Co, Edwin Southorn and Rowland Smitheman & Co. Production of pipes declined in the early twentieth century in the wake of cigars and cigarettes, whilst a tax on pipes further contributed to this downturn.

William Southorn founded his works in Broseley Wood in 1823, and the factory remained in production for 100 years (**45**). Southorn had two sons, Edwin and William, but there seems to have been a disagreement in the family. William, the younger son, took over from his father, whilst Edwin joined a rival, Noah Roden II, at his factory which was nearby in Benthall parish (on the site of the former Pitchyard Pottery). It was Edwin who was the most progressive: his factory was steam powered, his decoration included transfer-printed colours and enamelled mouth-pieces, whilst he invented water pipes, which had hollow water-filled bodies to cool the smoke down. Edwin died in 1876 and by 1881 his brother was running both factories, trading under the name William Southorn & Co. William not only took over Edwin's trade mark but the title 'Broseley Pipeworks'. Production at the Benthall factory, that had become known as the Raleigh Pipeworks, ended between 1895 and 1909.

The third factory was the Crown Pipeworks, established in King Street, Broseley in 1881, by Rowland Smitheman. It is possible that Smitheman moved into a gap in the market that emerged after the death of Edwin Southorn. Adverts suggest that he was making much the same range of pipes as Southorn's. After closure in 1917, the works was sold to William Southorn & Co in 1923, and remained in production on a small scale until 1960.

The early stages of pipe-making were similar to brick or tile manufacture in that the clay had to be prepared to make it plastic, for example by using a small pug mill. It was primarily a manual rather than a mechanised process and changed little over time. However, the development of factory production in the nineteenth century meant the demarcation of work into separate roles, whereas formerly the pipes had been made by the 'master'. In the latter stages of the industry most of the jobs were undertaken by women. By 1956 at the Crown Pipeworks there was a reversion to the earlier craft tradition, whereby Harry Southorn and his two female assistants undertook multiple roles.

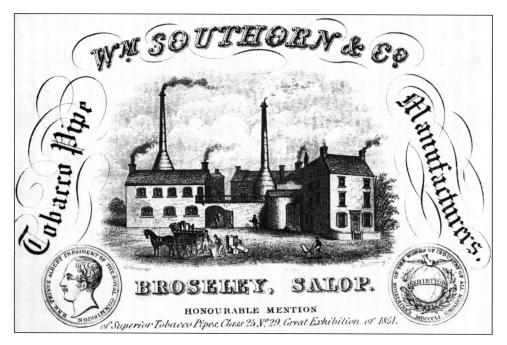

45 *William Southorn's tobacco pipeworks at Leggs Hill, Broseley Wood, was built in 1823 and was the earliest of the local pipe factories. The factory has been demolished but the house still stands*

After the clay had been prepared it was rolled into a 'dummy' in the approximate shape of a bowl and stem. The stem was threaded with a steel wire to make a draw hole and the dummy was put in a cast iron mould to press it into the exact shape. The inside of the bowl was hollowed out in a hand press. Afterwards the pipe was trimmed to remove the seams left by the mould, and the maker's stamp was impressed into the stem. The pipes were laid out in saggars and covered in china clay dust before being fired. The shorter-stemmed pipes were put in round saggars, and the longer-stemmed pipes in rectangular saggars. At the Crown Pipeworks the pipes were fired in a small kiln for about two days, using 2 tons of coal. The tips of the stems were dipped in enamel to make a mouthpiece, and the pipes were then ready for packing in cardboard boxes, also made at the works, before being despatched.

9
INDUSTRIAL COMMUNITIES

Ironbridge changed slowly from a rural to an industrial district, much more slowly than many of the industrial towns of the Midlands and the North. As a consequence, settlements evolved in a relatively haphazard fashion. In stark contrast to industrial towns where rows of monotonously regimented houses were erected in large developments, the scattered villages of Ironbridge were characterised by short rows or single cottages clustered together with no logical relationship to one another.

The earliest industrial workers lived in small cottages, often with workshops alongside. An early map of Jackfield, for example, shows small dwellings known as mughouses with kilns attached to them (**5**). These cottages, some of which have survived in a modernised form, usually had a single room downstairs with one or two sleeping chambers above in an attic lit by dormer windows, and perhaps a brewhouse lean-to at the back. The miners or potters who lived in them usually grew vegetables in their gardens and husbanded livestock in smallholdings. This tradition originated in the part-time nature of industrial work and the need for miners to supplement their income through agriculture — Abraham Darby I came from the same farmer-craftsman culture in the Black Country. The enduring manifestation of this national trait is the allotment. In the Severn Gorge it was also customary to keep pigs, which were butchered in the winter months. In fact in 1776, the agricultural journalist Arthur Young noted with satisfaction that there was 'not a door without a stone trough with the pig eating his supper'.

Our knowledge of housing in the eighteenth century is strongest in Coalbrookdale, where it was effectively controlled by the Coalbrookdale Company partners (**46**). Richard Ford was responsible for one of the earliest rows of cottages built for industrial workers. Tea Kettle Row in Coalbrookdale, situated just behind his own Rosehill House, was begun in 1735 and cottages were added to the row over a period to about 1746. It was a speculative venture by an ironmaster who knew he had a captive market: quality housing was a necessary inducement to encourage workers to settle in the coalfield, but was a lucrative form of income in its own right.

The small cottage of three or four rooms set the standard for housing the labouring classes. Terraces had a limited distribution, being confined principally to Coalbrookdale and the new industrial town of Coalport until the nineteenth century. Elsewhere, cottages were built singly or in pairs throughout the eighteenth century, continuing the tradition of the early industrial settlements. For many people, however, domestic standards fell far short of this. The Darby family and others did not invest in new houses where older buildings could be modified. The best example of this practice was at the site of the

46 *Nailers Row was the earliest of the rows of terraced houses in Coalbrookdale and was the result of piecemeal development in the early eighteenth century. The row is now demolished. Behind the row towers the Lincoln Hill quarry*

Upper Forge in Coalbrookdale, where a disused malthouse, an engine house, laundry, coach house and a seventeenth-century timber-framed house (once the home of Abraham Darby I) were all converted to tenements by the end of the eighteenth century. A similar story can be told elsewhere in the district. Two seventeenth-century charter-masters' houses, Bedlam Hall (see **23, colour plate 2**) and the Lloyds (**47**), endured the same fate, being divided up into tenements before their eventual demolition, the latter having been a hostel for railway navvies by 1861.

The early charter-masters' houses had been based on traditional farmhouses, but in the eighteenth century this class of dwelling entered the realm of polite architecture. For example, at Coalbrookdale Abraham Darby I and Richard Ford built Dale House and Rosehill House respectively, which are no different in their form and decoration from the Georgian town houses of Shrewsbury (**48**). Both stand within sight, sound and smell of the Coalbrookdale works. This was typical of the mercantile classes in the eighteenth century and in contrast to the nineteenth century, when it became unfashionable and unnecessary for the factory owner to build his house so near to his source of wealth.

The paternalistic hand of the Coalbrookdale ironmasters extended beyond the housing stock to control over food supplies. Shortages of food or punishing rises in the costs of provisions were a sporadic source of popular discontent in industrial Britain. The

47 *The Lloyds, a charter-master's house of the early seventeenth century, is shown here in a watercolour dated 1898, shortly before it was demolished. By this time the house was divided up into tenements*

first such riots in the Ironbridge area occurred after the bad harvest of 1756, when the Darby family and their property narrowly escaped attack from angry colliers, miners and bargemen. The Darby family outmanouvered potential malcontents by buying up farms in the district, which gave them adequate land on which to graze and rear working animals, and ensured that grain would not be sent away to markets in times of shortage. In Coalbrookdale, the Darbys erected a corn mill in about 1781, its waterwheel supplied with water from the pumping engine recycling water for the furnaces. In Benthall in the late eighteenth century, Edward Harries erected a corn mill with a waterwheel of so stupendous a diameter it became a tourist attraction (**colour plate 17**).

The population of the Ironbridge district was nevertheless small by industrial standards. Different social classes lived in close proximity to each other — witness, for example, the Darby family houses in Coalbrookdale and the neighbouring cottages — but enclosed communities produced their own tensions. As we have seen, the inhabitants often lived in short terraces or large tenemented buildings. In these crowded neighbourhoods partition walls were thin, while facilities for brewing and washing, and sometimes even cooking, were shared, giving a natural point of social contact and stressing the need for co-operation in daily life. Privacy in this environment was a rare commodity, especially when families took in lodgers to make up the rent, and when an average two-bedroom house would be expected to accommodate six people.

48 *Dale House, on the left, was built by Abraham Darby I, while Rosehill House, to its right, was built by Richard Ford. The houses overlooked the Upper Furnace Pool but the view was improved by planting trees and creating pleasure grounds. The iron bridge was first mentioned in 1801 but was demolished in 1849*

None of the workers' cottages had sanitation or running water; at the Upper Forge in Coalbrookdale, the tail race of the waterwheel doubled as a sewer. The wash house was traditionally known as a brewhouse, which betrays its origin in the tradition of domestic brewing. It provided an area large enough to accommodate the necessary array of wooden tubs and vats. Pigs were also butchered and salted in the brewhouse and then hung inside the house. The laundry was a female domain, one of the few they possessed, in a period when cleanliness was a moral issue. Poorer women or elderly widows were often obliged to 'take in' laundry from other working women. The fate of unmarried women was often to be washerwomen.

How much do we really know of domestic and private lives in an industrial village? The realities are difficult to penetrate, especially as contemporary evidence is largely filtered through the subjective eyes of the educated classes. The underprivileged have left comparatively little evidence behind of what they thought and did. A rare exception is the diary of Thomas Beard, written in the 1830s by a Jackfield barge owner but as prone to distortion as any other contemporary account. A catalogue of sexual misadventures, domestic violence and other personal tragedies gives a flavour of life in the raw:

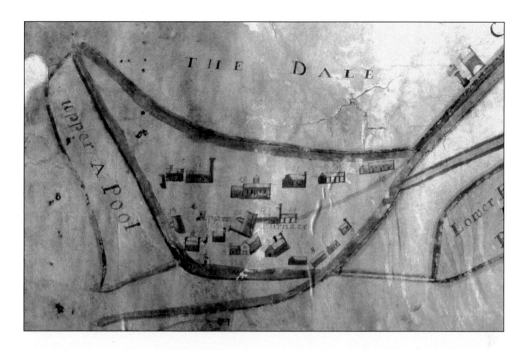

1   *Thomas Slaughter's map of Coalbrookdale, surveyed in 1753, is a valuable document to the archaeologist. This extract shows the Coalbrookdale Upper Works with its blast furnace, air furnaces and boring mills*

2   *Paul Sandby Munn's watercolour showing Bedlam Hall on the left, and the ironworks on the right, was drawn in 1802. It was strongly influenced by de Loutherbourg's 'Coalbrookdale by Night' (see 23)*

3 This portrait of William Reynolds was painted in 1795 as one of a series of portraits of leading ironmasters. Reynolds is holding a drawing of the iron aqueduct at nearby Longdon-on Tern, cast at Ketley in 1795 to Thomas Telford's design. The painting shows an inclined plane in the background

4 Edward Burney's view of the Iron Bridge appeared in Curiosities of England and Wales,
published in 1789. On the left of the picture is a team of bowhaulers pulling a trow

5 'An afternoon view of Coalbrookdale', painted by William Williams in 1777. In the distance are
the pools, buildings and coke hearths of the Coalbrookdale Works

6 *A print of 'the middle steam engine in the Dale' published by de Loutherbourg in 1805. It probably depicts the Resolution steam engine erected in 1781 by the Coalbrookdale Company to recycle water for its blast furnaces. Artistic licence is very much to the fore here*

7 *Ironstone mines in Madeley Wood, painted by Warington Smyth in 1847. The winding engines were of the Heslop type. On the right are women picking out the nodules of ironstone from the pit bank*

8   *The Coalport Warehouse was erected across the terminus of the Shropshire Canal, which acted as a transhipment point where goods were loaded on to Severn trows and barges*

9   *A Caughley jug in typical blue-and-white Chinese style, the pattern having been applied under the glaze by transfer printing. The lettering was painted on by hand*

10 *A teapot made at Walter Bradley's Pottery in the last decade of the eighteenth century. The factory is said to have been at Coalport, but its exact location is unknown*

11 *A view of Coalport painted on a Coalport vase, probably dating to 1810-14. The reverse of the vessel is signed by Thomas Baxter, a London decorator*

12 *The double-handled mug was a standard Coalport product. This example, for ornamental use, was made around 1830, and was hand-painted and gilded. It may have been commissioned as a commemorative piece by a playing-card manufacturer*

13 *A flower-encrusted 'Coalbrookdale' kettle, one of the characteristic Coalport products of the 1820s and 1830s, a style that occupied some of the factory's best painters*

14   *This special Peacock design was made at Maws Tileworks in 1928*

15   New printing techniques allowed tile manufacturers to produce colour catalogues, which became an important tool for marketing. The example here shows floor tiles and their suggested arrangement by Maw & Co

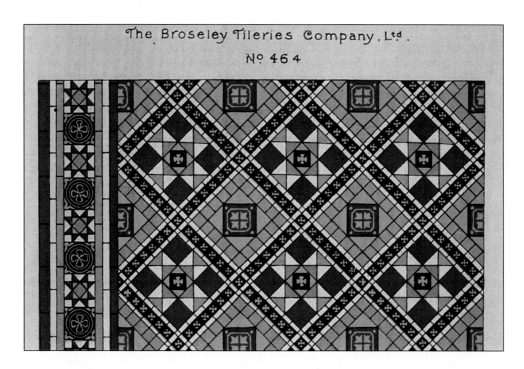

16   *Coloured tiles were cheap and easy to manufacture and could be arranged in endless geometrical patterns. These floor tiles are from the Broseley Tileries catalogue*

17   *The corn mill and its waterwheel at Benthall, erected by Edward Harries in the last decade of the eighteenth century, and drawn by Paul Sandby Munn in 1802. In the background, silhouetted against the sky, is a familiar horse gin for winding coal from a pit*

18 *The railway viaduct built in 1862–4 towers over the Coalbrookdale Upper Works. Below it are the tall closely spaced walls enclosing the waterwheel that powered the turning mill*

19 *The recreated dining room at Rosehill House in Coalbrookdale. The portraits of Alfred and Rebecca Darby were painted in 1848 on the occasion of their marriage*

20   The cast iron clock tower on the Great Warehouse at the Coalbrookdale Upper Works is a prominent landmark and an advert for the company's products. The clock tower was built in 1843, five years later than the warehouse

21   The Iron Bridge is the focal point of the district. On the north bank of the river is the Market Square with the church on the hill above it

22   The Wesleyan Infants School on Madeley Hill was opened in 1859 and is a showcase of the local brick and tile trade

23   The Hay Inclined Plane, viewed from the lower canal basin

24   The showroom at the Craven Dunnill Tileworks, now the Jackfield Tile Museum

25   Broseley Pipeworks has been restored as a time capsule, where the materials and tools of pipemaking have been reinstated, just as they were left, when the factory closed in 1960

24 March 1830, John Transom was Catchd in Bed with Another Man's Wife at Worcester By the Woman's Husband and the Man Stuck a Pickel in his Backside Which Caused him to Run away without his Clothes and after that offered the man 15 shillings to make it up.

17 March 1833, Jack Lowe beat his sweetheart & gave her 2 black eyes at the Calcutts.

11 April 1836, John Morgan's daughter Becky Morgan had a Bastard Born by a Young Man from Shrewsbury by Walter Faulk who Lodged there.

9 November 1836, Daniel Lloyd Gott over the small pox.

4 May 1838, Edward Harris missing out of Lumly's barge at Coalport, drunk, believed drowned in Severn.

21 May 1839, Adam Yates horsewhipt his wife Lidia untill she cried Murder for Getting Drunk at Jackfield.

Beard made several references to the outbreak of cholera in 1832, when '32 people have died of plague at Lincoln Hill since this day fortnight', and to the dangers of underground work: in 1836 '10 men burnt very bad at Meadow Pits, Madeley'. He also suggests that the River Severn claimed as many lives as the pits. Occasional references are made to trials at Shrewsbury Assizes, one of which concerned the trial in 1829 of John Noden for the rape of Elizabeth Cureton. Transcripts of the trial and of two subsequent appeals give us a valuable insight into the culture of ordinary men and women and contemporary attitudes to sexual relations.

The story is compelling in its own right, especially as it reveals individuals rather than a generic 'class'. Elizabeth Cureton was the daughter of a moulder at the Coalbrookdale works and was 24 years old when John Noden assaulted her in the parlour of her home at Tea Kettle Row. Noden was a 27-year-old odd-job man who lodged nearby and who had been pursuing Elizabeth for several years. At his trial Noden was found guilty, largely on the basis that he had incriminated himself, and was sentenced to hang.

Almost immediately Coalbrookdale appealed against the sentence, its campaign led by the local surgeon, Edward Edwards. Such appeals were not uncommon in the case of rape, a capital offence until 1832. Communities also dispensed their own form of justice independent of the law. Men who beat their wives, no less than women suspected of making false accusations, could expect to suffer the punishment of 'rough music'. Effigies of straw, known as mawkins, were burnt outside the perpetrator's door, having been taken there in a procession led by a cacophony of tin cans and whistles. It was a public shaming of the individual by the community. In Noden's case, two petitions were signed by over 350 people, including the local elite — the Darby family, the clergy and local surgeons — claiming a miscarriage of justice. Elizabeth Cureton suffered betrayal and humiliation at the hands of her neighbours and doctor, even from people who hardly knew her.

It became one of the largest appeal cases of the 1820s. Although the conviction stood (the Law was Elizabeth Cureton's most steadfast supporter), Noden was transported to Bermuda, returning to Coalbrookdale in 1854. As a later local diarist Charles Peskin noted, the 'returned convict' died there in 1873. We do not know what happened to Elizabeth Cureton. Two women of that name were married in the district in the early 1830s.

Statements given to the appeal reveal much about Elizabeth Cureton's sexual history, in a manner that suggests that she had done nothing unusual and was not especially promiscuous. At 24 years old, an unmarried artisan's daughter could still expect to attract a husband in the same social class, and in the meantime she enjoyed a certain amount of sexual freedom. Although industrial Shropshire was sexually more conformist than rural Shropshire, sexual norms were influenced by the habits of the lower working classes, the forge women who 'enter beer shops, call for their pints and smoke their pipes like men'. During the appeal, five men came forward claiming to have had sexual relations with Elizabeth. Although they all fled as soon as they suspected she was pregnant (the surgeon Edwards told the court that she had previously suffered a miscarriage), Elizabeth had been able to bestow favours on whom she chose by controlling the practice of night-visiting.

The ritual of night-visiting grew out of live-in labour on farms, but remained prevalent in industrial Shropshire where young adults still lived with their parents and where space was at a premium. Parents co-operated by disappearing to bed, allowing women to receive their suitors privately. Favour was apparently symbolised by the custom of offering wine. In this way women were able to conduct their affairs on their own terms and without secrecy — courtship could never be less than semi-public in closely packed communities.

A more public arena for courtship was the fair or wake, where Elizabeth Cureton met the majority of her sexual partners. Here women dallied while men showed off their prowess in animal-baiting. At the Ironbridge, Broseley and Oakengates wakes, bull baiting and cock fighting were common sports but were routinely condemned by local elites as an example of working-class vulgarity and gratuitous bloodlust. Both sports were dying out under local pressure in the 1830s and were made illegal in 1835, although workers could still enjoy prize fighting, and were eager spectators at public executions into the 1840s. The wakes, like public houses, were damned as places of drunken excess and barbarism, and were a focus of class conflicts that grew up in industrialised Shropshire.

The ironmasters could not afford, as we can, the luxury of sympathising with the behaviour of the colliers and ironworkers; but with hindsight the conflict between the two groups seems to have been inevitable. Iron and coal were highly capitalised industries. Pre-eminence in the iron trade was won by ploughing profits back into businesses, which fostered a culture of frugality and self-discipline. Iron and coal were also dangerous occupations that relied on a disciplined workforce. In such circumstances, the unruly behaviour of off-duty workers, and their profligacy with money, naturally horrified their employers. The focus of this horror was usually the public house, although not from any disapproval of beer. Indeed the public house was an integral part of industrial life. Some friendly societies and benefit clubs met there and charter-masters were often publicans who expected colliers to buy drinks on credit while they waited for their pay.

Colliers were renowned for excessive consumption after the fortnightly reckoning, followed by begging and borrowing before the next reckoning. Those who had a vested moral or political interest may have exaggerated this way of life, but it was certainly a common phenomenon. As the Poor Law Commissioners were told in 1835, 'the great evil with colliers is, they over-stimulate themselves by their irregular habits of living . . . with many it is either a feast or a fast'.

49 *Jackfield church was built in 1759 to serve the local industrial population, but suffered structural problems as a result of mining subsidence. It was superseded by a new church in 1863 and was demolished about 1960*

However, when the dangers of the work are remembered, the apparent recklessness of colliers and the like can be seen in a more realistic context. The majority of colliers had known or even witnessed the death or disablement of a fellow worker, and to such people a brawl, a cock fight or a public hanging may not have seemed so shockingly brutal as they would today. In 1785 the La Rochefoucauld brothers were surprised to hear that the ironworkers did not save any of their money for old age, until they were told that an ironworker did not expect to get old. This is a slight exaggeration as many men contributed to Friendly Societies for their future welfare, but it reveals an underlying truth: years of hard labour wore men down slowly, although such cumulative effects did not make headlines in the way that pit disasters did. The circumstances of industrial life may help to explain extreme behaviour as a form of psychological release. In this respect, the public house performed an important social function dissipating the tensions of industrial work, ironically in a similar way to the chapel.

In the eighteenth and early nineteenth centuries, the higher aspirations of the labouring classes were most commonly expressed in terms of religion. The established church was traditionally weak in newly industrialised districts, and Shropshire was no exception, where the churches of Madeley, Broseley and Benthall were inconveniently located for the new industrial workforce. A church was erected at Jackfield in 1759 (**49**), and a church was built in Ironbridge in 1837. The latter was largely government-funded and was known as a Commissioners' Church. It was part of a one million pound scheme initiated in 1818 to build new churches in ill-served industrial districts to combat growing atheism and non-conformism. The Church Commissioners also awarded a grant to the building of a church in Coalbrookdale in 1851.

Non-conformist groups, at first chiefly Baptists and Methodists, exploited the tardiness of the established church in evangelising the industrial districts. Non-conformist Christianity provided a powerful emotional release for the workers and, within a religious community, an artisan or labourer could also achieve status and command a respect from his peers that might not be so forthcoming in the workplace.

It should also be remembered that the masters as well as the men could eschew the Establishment. The Darby and Reynolds families were members of the Society of Friends, one of the oldest established groups of Dissenting Christians. It was founded in the mid-seventeenth century and, following the Civil War, was spectacularly successful in converting new members. It soon established a stronghold in the commercial and maritime centre of Bristol, the Quaker community into which Abraham Darby I moved at the turn of the eighteenth century.

'Quaker' was originally a derogatory nickname, derived from their practice of quaking and trembling in the presence of God. Although many Quakers, like the Darby and Reynolds families, or the Barclay family of banking fame, amassed considerable fortunes and influence during the industrial revolution, their egalitarian outlooks, frugal lifestyles and enthusiasm for social reform made them outsiders. Moreover, in British culture old money is always better than new. The Quaker industrialists of Coalbrookdale were tradesmen; it took time for them to be accepted as gentlemen.

The Quakers established themselves at Broseley in the 1670s, but in the eighteenth century their meetings were transferred to Coalbrookdale where they remained until 1954. Nevertheless, Quakerism was not likely to have been the religious experience of Darby employees. Amongst the labouring classes, Methodism was dominant. It was founded by John Wesley (1703–91) in Bristol in 1739, after which he and his brother Charles became itinerant preachers across Britain and America, making several visits to industrial Shropshire (John Wesley even saw the future Iron Bridge laid out on the river bank ready for erection).

The leading figure in Shropshire's Methodist movement was John Fletcher (**50**). Fletcher was born in Geneva in 1729 and migrated to Britain in 1752. After his Evangelical conversion, he made contacts with John and Charles Wesley and was ordained curate of Madeley church in 1757. He became vicar in 1760 and remained there until his death in 1785, where he devoted his energies to the problems of an industrial parish.

Fletcher oversaw the building of a Methodist chapel in Madeley Wood, in the industrial heartland of his parish. A second chapel at Coalbrookdale was begun in 1784. After his death, Fletcher's wife Mary continued to hold religious meetings in a barn next to the vicarage and preached in the Madeley Wood and Coalbrookdale chapels. Fletcher's charismatic leadership drew Evangelically minded Christians from a wide area and earned Madeley parish the epithet 'Mecca of Methodism', although its Methodism was

50 *John Fletcher (1729–85), vicar of Madeley for 25 years, was one of the most charismatic leaders of the Methodist movement*

rather loosely defined and the word really only described someone of strong religious feelings. Its correspondingly loose organisation was also the root of numerous schisms. In industrial Shropshire the most prominent sub-sect was the Methodist New Connexion founded by Alexander Kilham in 1797.

Most of the non-conformist denominations, while rejecting the pomp and ceremony of the Church of England, nevertheless elevated their godliest preachers to cult status. Methodist ministers such as Samuel Taylor, who came to Shropshire in 1798, were charismatic figures whose sermons were highly charged with emotion, characteristics that still distinguish successful preachers such as Billy Graham. The power of preaching was necessary to maintain religious fervour in denominations whose demands on their followers were difficult to live up to. Men and women could be expected to uphold strict and often unrealistic morals. The inhibitions inherent in these morals prevented normal sexual lives, while their attitudes to sin could effectively cut them off from the outside world. The consequence was that Methodism suffered alternating periods of revival and inertia. One such revival took place during the difficult years of the trade slump following the end of war with France in 1815, but the ardour cooled when prosperity returned in the 1820s; others, such as the revival of the 1830s, seem not to have been conditioned by economic factors.

The fervour of religious experience can be gleaned from many sources, such as the following account, about a Primitive Methodist meeting held in 1839 on the north side of the coalfield at Wrockwardine Wood Chapel, where

> The Lord in answer to united prayer, so filled the Chapel with His glorious presence that the congregation was shaken throughout. The speaking was powerful, and it went on well until sinners were brought into such deep distress of soul on account of their lost state, that we were obliged to turn it into a prayer meeting. The most distressing cries for mercy were very soon heard from every part of the chapel . . . so that there was full employment for all who knew the Lord . . . eighteen or twenty precious souls obtained a solid sense of sins forgiven, and were delivered from sin and Satan's power; and near that number found the like blessing at the other forms and others went away in distress. This has been a great day.

In the late eighteenth century, the Coalbrookdale Company established two Charity (i.e. free) Schools in Coalbrookdale to provide elementary education, but this was exceptional in its benevolence. The chapel was the likeliest source of education for children until the mid-nineteenth century when National Schools were built with funds from private benefactors. Provision of children's education was of course constrained by their employment in the local industries, although the parents who sent them there had often themselves experienced work at an early age. John Fletcher established one of the first schools for children in Madeley in addition to the Sunday schools, with the intention of inculcating morality and piety in addition to the skills of reading and writing. But these early schools were not necessarily sympathetic to children's needs, tending to castigate rather than celebrate childhood. Even the godly Fletcher found children's games foolish

51 *The Coalbrookdale Literary and Scientific Institution was built in 1859 and was one of the first buildings to be built of blue bricks. It is now a youth hostel*

and full of mischief and thought children would be better off without them. The last thing children needed after six day's hard work was the penury of Sunday school.

In the climate of self-help fostered by non-conformism came some remarkable adult institutions, like the Madeley Church Instruction Society and the Broseley Literary Society. Autodidacts were common in industrial Britain. Dickens recognised the type in his novel of industrial England, *Hard Times*, where he speaks of men who through 'their broken pieces of leisure through many years . . . mastered difficult sciences, and acquired a knowledge of most unlikely things'. In 1853 the Coalbrookdale Literary and Scientific Institution was founded, and six years later was given a building at the expense of the Coalbrookdale Company that contained a library and lecture hall, art studio and concert room (**51**). A similar institution was founded in Madeley in 1868 for the employees of the Madeley Wood Company.

The industrial revolution brought a degree of fluidity in the social structure that enabled a minority of artisans to succeed as entrepreneurs, although it may have taken generations to achieve it. The most famous was the Guest family of Broseley, who emigrated to South Wales and eventually at Dowlais controlled Britain's largest ironmaking company in the nineteenth century, known today as Guest, Keen & Nettlefold (GKN). But the Guests are an exceptional case. It should also be remembered that, far from being a homogenous group, the working class had its own hierarchy. The aristocrats of the local working class were probably the painters at the Coalport Chinaworks, whose workshops produced many talented men whose achievements were equally laudable. In a male-dominated society, women could be painters, but were rigidly excluded from being gilders and appear to have flourished less well in other intellectual pursuits. The nature of the work was conducive to talk and Coalport men were noted for their appetite for political debate. Others nurtured their artistic talents. Charles Muss learned his craft at Caughley and eventually left Coalport for London, where he regularly exhibited paintings at the Royal Academy, and turned to enamel painting on metal for patrons including George IV. Another of the Coalport painters, whose speciality was bird painting and who worked there until he was about 70, was John Randall (c1810–1910). Randall was the first historian of industrial Shropshire, writing histories of both Madeley and Broseley. In the social environment of the nineteenth century the ability of men to rise from nothing to lead creative lives was a remarkable achievement.

10
COALBROOKDALE

In 1801 the Bath clergyman Richard Warner described Coalbrookdale as a valley 'hemmed in by high rocky banks, finely wooded', which 'would be exceedingly picturesque, were it not for the huge founderies, which, volcano like, send up volumes of smoke into the air'. Acts of Parliament have reduced the emissions of smoke, but the contrast between the greenery of its wooded slopes and the sprawling Coalbrookdale Foundry in the Dale has hardly changed since then.

The Coalbrookdale Foundry, occupying what used to be known as the Lower Works, has been in continuous production since Abraham Darby built a blast furnace there in 1715. Iron may not have been smelted there since the early nineteenth century, but for the past 200 years its cupola furnaces have melted pig and scrap iron for a wide repertoire of cast iron products. The Iron Bridge was probably cast there in the eighteenth century; in the nineteenth century it gained a reputation for cast iron gates and other ornamental work, and today it produces parts for Aga and Rayburn cookers.

Immediately above the Coalbrookdale Foundry, and the centrepiece of Coalbrookdale's heritage, is the former Upper Works, now a large open space surrounded by buildings on three sides and a viaduct on the fourth. The viaduct, built in 1862–4, is still used by trains taking coal to Ironbridge Power Station (**colour plate 18**). At the northern end of the site, and at a lower level than the remainder, is the nucleus of the small ironworks where Abraham Darby made his breakthrough in smelting iron in 1709. The blast furnace was among the first industrial monuments to be restored, a campaign to prevent its demolition having triumphed in 1959 when the site was cleared of foundry waste and opened as a small museum to celebrate the 250th anniversary of coke smelting.

The blast furnace is very well protected inside a steel and glass cover building. Of the original blast furnace on the site little is now visible, although the stone charging platform behind the furnace was built with it. On the cast iron lintels spanning the openings to the furnace are the initials BEW and EWB, which have never been satisfactorily explained (**52**). The essential problem with them is that they have not been related to any individual known to have been connected with the furnace. They might refer to the Brooke family, who owned the land on which the furnace was built until it was taken from them in the civil war. Alternatively they might refer to the lessee who built the furnace, or the initials might be nothing more than the graffiti of moulders who worked there, a practice not unknown in the area. The accompanying date of 1638 is an error introduced by previous restoration work. It should read 1658. The latter is the most likely date for the erection of the furnace. An inscription on one of the other lintels refers to the rebuilding of the furnace in 1777 by Abraham Darby III, and the brick structure we see today belongs to this date.

The blast furnace does not survive to its original height, although its mode of operation can be easily understood. The furnace was charged with raw materials at the top, from the charging platform behind the furnace. At the base of the furnace are two large openings with the inscribed lintels. The openings were later blocked with brick, but the opening at the side, under the 1777 inscription, was the forehearth where the furnace was tapped (**52**). Originally, a building stood here known as the casting house, and was where molten iron was run into pig beds or where it was run into a large cauldron from which ladles were filled to cast smaller items in casting boxes. The other large opening was for the tuyère. Originally the furnace was blown using a pair of giant bellows, each about 20ft (6.1m) long and housed inside another building (the bellows house), but these were replaced by cast iron cylinders, operating much like a bicycle pump, in the 1770s. The use of a cylinder allowed greater distribution of air into the furnace and in fact another, smaller tuyère opening was added on the opposite side of the furnace, in a passage below the charging platform. The remaining, blank side of the furnace was where the waterwheel was situated. Over time, at least three wheels worked in the pit, the latest of which was said by one visitor to have been 30ft (9.15m) in diameter. Score marks can be seen where one of the waterwheels scraped against the wheelpit wall.

The significance of the furnace in the history of the industrial revolution has overshadowed the remainder of the features at the Upper Works, which together form one of the best preserved eighteenth-century ironworks in Britain. Behind the blast furnace and its charging platform are a high dam and the Upper Furnace Pool. The pool is at the confluence of two streams, but its close proximity to the works is unusual and was not ideal. On at least two occasions, c1705 and 1801, floods caused water to flow over the top of the dam, causing considerable damage.

A few yards away from the blast furnace, and also built against the dam wall, is the snapper furnace, the only example of its kind still standing (**53**). It is known to have been under construction by 1794, but there is no evidence that it was ever finished or used. A snapper furnace was a small blast furnace used to supplement output in times of high demand. Snappers were common among Shropshire ironworks in the late eighteenth century but are not known outside the area. A snapper furnace could smelt 10-15 tons of pig iron a week, at a time when an average Shropshire furnace produced up to 30 tons a week, but when the new blast furnaces in South Wales were producing around 50 tons a week. It is difficult to envisage how the Coalbrookdale snapper could have worked because a stone wall has been built over the top of it. If the structure was ever complete, it would have stood considerably higher than it does today. Like the blast furnace it has two openings, one for the forehearth and the other for the tuyère.

On the opposite side of the Upper Works, and beneath the railway viaduct, are the ruins of a former turning mill (**colour plate 18**). A mill was probably built here in the 1720s and was where the first engine cylinders were bored. After 1734, when a patent restricting the manufacture of steam engines expired, the company built a new boring mill further down the valley near the Upper Forge and the mill at the Upper Works became secondary to it. The structures that survive today are a later rebuilding by Abraham Darby III, probably in the 1770s. Two high brick walls enclose the wheelpit. In 1803 the waterwheel was described as being 28ft (8.55m) in diameter. The mill was used for boring

52 *In its present form, the blast furnace at the Coalbrookdale Upper Works dates from its rebuilding in 1777 by Abraham Darby III*

53 *The Coalbrookdale snapper furnace is the only surviving snapper furnace in Shropshire. Designed for smelting additional amounts of iron in times of high demand, the furnace was 'unfinished' in 1794 and was probably never blown in*

steam pipes and for turning, which means smoothing and polishing the outsides of the engine cylinders. Neither of these latter operations required the same precision as boring the cylinders in which the pistons worked. The buildings continued in use as workshops in the late nineteenth century, and were dwarfed when the viaduct was built in 1862–4. Beneath the viaduct are the partial remains of other small workshops.

There is a sharp contrast between the scale of the early buildings at the Upper Works — the furnaces and the turning mill — and the buildings of the later nineteenth century. The middle of the site is now grass and tarmac, where stands a 'boy and swan' fountain cast by the Coalbrookdale Company for the Great Exhibition in 1851, but was at one time occupied by a jumble of small workshops. The later buildings reflect the increase in scale in the engineering trades in the nineteenth century. The eponymously named Long Warehouse houses the IGMT library and the Ironbridge Institute. It was built at some time between 1883 and 1902, and its lower storey is open-fronted because it had railways passing through it, with goods loaded on to wagons from the floors above. Hidden behind it is a large shed characterised by its asymmetrical gabled bays, which was a large engineering and enamelling shop built at about the same time. Opposite the Long Warehouse is the Great Warehouse now housing the Museum of Iron. It was built in 1838 (the date is cast on one of the iron columns inside the building) when the lease of the site was renewed and the Coalbrookdale Company decided to concentrate on casting ornamental work. The building is a fine example of the local industrial vernacular with its original cast iron glazing bars to the windows and wide doorways through which a railway passed. The cast iron clock tower was added in 1843, an appropriate advert for the company (**colour plate 20**). Originally it had cast iron swans at the bases of the four corners.

South of the Great Warehouse are the former offices of the Coalbrookdale Company, built in the late nineteenth century on the site of earlier buildings, and next to it a yard entered through fine iron gates cast at the works. Beyond, in the yard, is the long brick engineering shop erected in 1879 and enlarged a few years later. This building replaced the older workshops at the Upper Works: It is now the Enginuity interactive design and technology centre.

There is plenty to explore and appreciate in Coalbrookdale outside the Upper Works. Up the hill beyond the Upper Furnace Pool is a small neighbourhood of houses that grew up in the eighteenth century (see **48**). The first large house is Dale House, begun by Abraham Darby I but not completed before his death in 1717. Originally it was two storeys with an attic, as can be seen in an engraving made in 1758 (see **7**), where the extent of its landscape garden can also be recognised. Its present appearance is the result of a substantial remodelling in the late eighteenth or early nineteenth century. Immediately uphill from it is Richard Ford's Rosehill House of the 1720s. Both Rosehill House and Dale House are fine early Georgian brick houses that mark a move away from the traditional timber framing in local buildings. Moreover, their symmetrical fronts introduced an ordered plan to the houses in contrast to the traditional houses that were unevenly planned around a great hall (as has survived at Madeley Court and Benthall Hall). Dale House and Rosehill House both have rooms restored to their eighteenth-century appearance (**colour plate 19**). Their respective coach houses also survive. The Dale House coach house stands at the bottom of the hill and is now a vehicle repair shop, but a mounting block survives outside.

Richard Ford built Tea Kettle Row, which stands above Rosehill House, as a speculative venture to house his workers. Looking closely, it is easy to see that it was a piecemeal development while its dormer windows, denoting attic rooms, are characteristic of the mid-eighteenth century. A Friends Meeting House which stood a little further uphill was unfortunately demolished in the 1960s, but on the hillside behind it is a burial ground with characteristically modest memorials to dead Darbys and their fellow Quakers, men such as William and Richard Reynolds.

On the other side of the Upper Works is a second, well-preserved row of houses known as Carpenters Row. These were built in the early 1780s and each originally consisted of four rooms. Unlike Tea Kettle Row, the houses have a full upper storey and many of them retain their original glazing and shutters. Vegetable plots were laid out in front of the houses, but the sense of them was lost when the track at the front was widened to a road (the original road ran through the works). Behind Carpenters Row are the nineteenth-century houses of Coalbrookdale, picturesquely scattered and some with characteristic iron-frame windows and cast iron lintels to the openings. They include a former school and a mill built by the Coalbrookdale Company, both now converted to dwellings (**54**).

54 *The former mill at Coalbrookdale has typical cast iron window frames, lintels and sills. It was built c1821 and had a waterwheel in the centre of it. It was converted to houses in the mid-1930s. On the left is the former Coalbrookdale school*

Another early row of houses here, known as Engine Row, recalls the Resolution engine, which was installed nearby to recycle water from the Boring Mill Pool to the Upper Furnace Pool.

The Grove Inn was licensed in 1839 as The Commercial Hotel and was later purchased by the Coalbrookdale Company. Further down the hill, the Methodist chapel and Anglican church stand close to each other. The chapel was built in 1890, replacing an earlier chapel, with an imposing Italianate front facing the road. Once it could accommodate 900 souls but it is no longer a religious building and now houses workshops. The church was designed by the partnership of Reeves and Voysey and was completed in 1854, but is not an especially distinguished example of Gothic Revival architecture. Ironically its chief benefactor was Abraham Darby IV, who was baptised in 1851, signalling a move to the established Church and away from the anti-establishment credentials of his Quaker forbears. In the graveyard are a number of cast iron grave markers.

The Coalbrookdale Youth Hostel was built in 1859 as the Literary and Scientific Institution (see **51**), one of the earliest instances of the use of blue bricks in the locality, and has fine cast iron entrance gates. Further down the Dale is the Upper Forge, one of the most important survivals of the Coalbrookdale iron industry, although its present guise — a mill and stable — is a little misleading, and its isolation belies its original setting in a busy industrial and domestic enclave (**55**).

54 *The Upper Forge was built in 1776 and was initially intended to be a slitting mill. It was subsequently used for the stamping and potting process and was converted to a mill and stables in the 1830s. The upper storeys of the mill are the result of a recent reconstruction*

The site relied on water power, but the Upper Forge Pool, uphill and on the opposite side of the road, is now infilled and occupied by buildings of the Coalbrookdale Foundry. An Upper Forge had stood here since at least 1668, standing at right angles to the surviving building and demolished in the 1930s when the road was widened. The surviving building was built in 1776, and was originally intended to be a slitting mill, where wrought iron bars were passed through rollers and were formed into rods of equal length. This plan was quickly abandoned and the building was converted for use in the refining of pig into wrought iron, using the stamping and potting method. Initially, the main parts of the process were undertaken in the older Upper Forge, with the new building simply housing a large hammer for drawing the iron bars into the finished shape ready for sale.

In 1785 the company expanded its operations. The new building was extended for the addition of a beam engine by adding a tall range at the end, later converted to a mill. From inside, it is easy to see the thick bob wall on which the engine's beam pivoted. The engine powered blowing cylinders, which were used to blow the finery hearths in the first part of the process. At the back of the building was a waterwheel powering the hammer for shingling the blooms taken from the hearths. The remainder of the stamping and potting process was carried out at the older Upper Forge.

Stamping and potting was given up at some time in the early nineteenth century, although the exact date is not known. The Upper Forge complex was later used as stabling for the company's numerous horses, while the engine house was converted to a mill for grinding the feed for the horses. This was water-powered and the wheelpit survives at the back of the building, as does the cast iron pipe that brought water from the Upper Forge Pool. Excavations behind the building also revealed the earlier wheelpits of the forge, along with the culverts, or tail races, which channelled the water into the Boring Mill pool that was immediately downhill from here but is now infilled.

Although the boring mill does not survive, a row of four timber-framed houses that stood in front of it, known as Rose Cottages (see **6**), stand as the earliest testimony to Coalbrookdale's iron trade. Until they were restored in the early 1970s, one of the cottages bore the date 1642. They were created for the workmen of the nearby forges and a steelworks built between here and the Upper Forge, but the building itself is even older, having probably been a barn and built in the sixteenth century.

The woods surrounding Coalbrookdale are worthy of exploration in their own right, not merely as picturesque and quiet diversions from the main attractions, but as an integral part of the historic landscape. The steeply sloped woods on either side of the Museum of Iron and foundry, known as Dale Coppice and Captain's Coppice, are ancient coppiced woodlands. In these woods the underwood was used for making charcoal, the only available fuel for smelting iron in the seventeenth century, and remaining an essential component of making wrought iron until the mid-eighteenth century. One of the subtle features of these woods are the old charcoal platforms, small and level clearings, on which the underwood was piled and charred. Upstream from the Upper Furnace Pool are similar woods alongside the two streams that converge to make the pool. The stream on the east side of the pool cannot be followed for some distance as it flows underground, but further upstream is the New Pool, which was used as a reservoir for the blast furnace below and is thought to have been created about 1698. From here a path continues alongside the stream, and, although it was straightened in the nineteenth century, it is essentially the line of an early railway between Coalbrookdale and the Coalbrookdale Company's other works at Lightmoor and Horsehay. At the end of the path are substantial remains of the Lightmoor Brickworks, the visible structures of which belong to the twentieth century and where production ceased in the 1980s.

The highlight of the woodland walks is the paths created in the late eighteenth century specifically for the well being of the workers in Coalbrookdale by Richard Reynolds. They begin at the top of the hill above Dale Coppice. From Church Road one path led north through the woods to a Doric temple, which has unfortunately now gone. The other path follows the ridge and ends at the foundations of an old Rotunda that had a colonnade of cast iron pillars. Immediately below here were the limestone caverns of Lincoln Hill, now long gone and overgrown, above which the Rotunda was precipitously sited, which may explain its demolition as early as 1804. The Rotunda offers the most spectacular views of the Ironbridge Gorge to be had without the aid of a balloon (**56**). From here the banks of the Severn rise steeply in thick woodland, and the focal point of the landscape is the Iron Bridge spanning the river.

56 *One of the best views of the Iron Bridge and the Severn Gorge is from the Rotunda on Lincoln Hill. The Rotunda stood at the end of one of Reynolds' Sabbath Walks but was taken down in 1804. Parts of its brick foundations are still visible*

11
IRONBRIDGE

The town of Ironbridge, as its name suggests, developed following the construction of the Iron Bridge in 1779. Before that time there were two small settlements, one at each end of the town. To the north east was The Green, centred around the Golden Ball public house, licensed in 1728. This was part of Madeley Wood, an area of woodland and common pasture where mining had been carried out since the medieval period. Settlement consisted of a scattering of small cottages, but with two large houses close to the river, Bedlam Hall and the Lloyds, both now demolished, which were reached by narrow lanes leading down from The Green (see **23, 47, colour plate 2**). The second settlement was dispersed along the wharf side from Dale End, at the lower end of Coalbrookdale, to the ferry crossing which the Iron Bridge replaced.

The Iron Bridge is, and always has been, the focus of the town (see **20**). The character of the single-span cast iron bridge derives from the five elegant ribs, the radials and connecting members, and the circles and ogee arched panels in the spandrels. The ramped deck has parapets of thin cast iron railings (**57**). The abutments are of stone, on the north side containing a narrow arch over a towpath. The two smaller cast iron arches beyond the south abutment were added in 1821 and replaced wooden arches, which themselves replaced a massive stone-faced embankment. The bridge has always been at the mercy of the underlying geology, which has tended to squeeze the abutments together. In 1974, major engineering works involved building an inverted arch underwater, so that the bridge was able to withstand much greater lateral pressure. After the Iron Bridge was opened, it was run by the Madeley Turnpike Trust and the brick toll-house on the south end is now a small museum.

The commercial centre of Ironbridge is immediately north of the bridge and was purposely planned by the turnpike trustees, the architecture of the buildings reflecting their status (**colour plate 21**). Facing it is the Tontine Hotel, built in 1780 by the Shrewsbury architect, John Hiram Haycock. It was extended to the east around 1786 by Samuel Wright of Kidderminster. The hotel with its assembly rooms not only provided accommodation for travellers and the many visitors to the area, but also acted as a focus for local industrialists. For example, the committee meetings of the Shropshire Canal Company were held there for many years. The three-storey building, of three bays extended to five, is typical of Georgian Shropshire with its hipped roof, windows with wedge lintels, and central pedimented doorcase. The hotel forms the west side of the market square, a raised area bound by a retaining wall, which is now a car park. Markets were held here weekly on a Friday, and in the nineteenth century it was a venue for fairs.

57 *The Iron Bridge was erected in 1779, as recorded on the cast iron parapet at the apex of the bridge*

At the back of the square is the five-bay market hall, formerly open-fronted with large round arches, now infilled and containing shops. The storeys above contain an advanced central bay, tall recessed arches, and tripartite sash windows to the centre and sides. A former bank is to the left, of rusticated stone, with a decorative eaves cornice. On the east side of the square is a smaller market building with four infilled arches.

Opposite the Market Square and next to the bridge is a large square three-storey shop with hipped roof and cast iron lintels, built in the early nineteenth century. There is a tunnel beneath to the river, which was used for bringing in provisions from trows and barges. A passage next to the building leads down to a riverside path, from which there is a good view of the bridge. Small cottages line the north side of this path.

Set up on the hillside is the Church of St Luke, the date stone laid in 1835 and completed in 1837. It is by the builder-architect, Thomas Smith of Madeley, and was funded by the Church Commissioners. A low-budget work, it is constructed of yellow brick with three pairs of tall, pointed arched windows to each side. Although it is generally plain in style, the church has particularly good cast iron windows with diamond glazing. Unusually, the tower, which incorporates the porch, is at the east end and the chancel is at the west end. The nature of the underlying geology is said to have dictated this. Inside the church is a three-sided gallery on cast iron columns, in much the same style as a non-conformist chapel, designed to accommodate as many people as possible — it was said in 1851 to seat 1662. The east window is by Evans of Shrewsbury. A long flight of steps leads up to the church from the Market Square and passes underneath the graveyard. This may follow the line of a path which predates the church.

The High Street is lined with Georgian and Victorian buildings, many retaining good period shop fronts. On the north side of the roundabout is a four-bay building with round-headed windows, which has a double shop front with inlaid tile decoration. To the south east, at the end of Waterloo Street, is the unusual Police Station and Court-House, in Italianate style and of blue brick with Grinshill stone and white brick dressings and open arches to the front. It was built in 1862 by Samuel Nevett, a local builder and architect.

Running uphill from the roundabout towards the north east is Madeley Road, constructed in 1810, and leading to The Green, the original settlement of the area. There are a few public buildings of note along its route: on the left is the Parochial Infants School of 1831. In Gothic style and of one storey on a plinth, the central bay is advanced and gabled. Further up the hill is a group of Wesleyan buildings. On the right is the very distinctive Wesleyan Infants School in polychrome brickwork, dated 1858, and by James Wilson of Bath (**colour plate 22**). It has Gothic windows and an Italianate bell-tower. On the side of the tower facing the road is a memorial to John Fletcher. Within its grounds is a former Methodist preaching-house, erected by Fletcher in 1777 (though altered) and doubling as a school. It is a single-storey brick building with gabled front, three-window sides and round headed openings. Behind these buildings is the area formerly known as The Green, including the Golden Ball public house. A new chapel was built on the opposite side of the road in 1837, designed by Samuel Smith of Madeley, and now converted to a house. It is of yellow brick with three-bay gabled front, pilasters, central doorcase and cast iron windows. Next to it is Belmont Road. There are some seventeenth- and eighteenth-century cottages along here, an extension of the settlement of The Green. They can be picked out because they are small, generally of one storey, with steeply pitched roofs, and retain dormer windows. At the end of these cottages is the rather grander Belmont House, constructed in 1753, now two dwellings. It is of two storeys and five bays with heavy window surrounds and large wedge lintels. A cartouche over the doorway reads P, and, on the line below, I M. To whom these initials belong has remained a mystery.

Further up Madeley Road is Orchard Lane, at the top of which is the former Woodlands Brick and Tile Works. The only surviving building is the office, now converted to a house, of white brick with decorated roof tiles, a moulded tile frieze, and circular stacks with barley twist decoration — a good advert for the company's products. In the far distance on top of the hill and overlooking the Gorge stands the former Madeley Union Workhouse, now Beeches Hospital. It has bell-towers and Gothic-style windows.

The hillside rising steeply above Ironbridge has a network of narrow lanes and alleyways which are best explored on foot. Though they were laid out before the development of Ironbridge in 1780, many of the buildings lining them are nineteenth-century in date. The middle-class Victorian villas in Gothic, or occasionally Classical, style are set out haphazardly in their own grounds. One of their most striking features is the variety in the colour and detail of their brickwork — for good reason, as many of them were built by managers in the local brick and tile industry. A notable example is the Gothic-style Orchard House, probably built around 1843 by John Davies, who owned a small brickworks in Jackfield with his brother. It is asymmetrical, with steep gables, barley-twist chimney shafts, and flat-headed windows with decorative glazing. It is constructed upon a high stone retaining wall, which supports a folly — a circular turret in polychrome brickwork. East of Orchard House is Southside pleasure grounds, formerly belonging to a house of the same name, a small steep garden open to the public. A circular summer-house with seating is located at mid-level and there is a good view looking down over the River Severn.

Not far from the church on St. Luke's Road is the former National School with integral master's house. Like the Police Station, it was built by Samuel Nevett, in 1859. Constructed of the same blue brick with pale stone dressings, it is Tudor-Gothic in style with two-light windows containing cast iron glazing and a central bell-tower. The front faces south and is visible from the opposite side of the river. The east gable stack is wide with multiple shafts and a frieze of blue-and-white brick decoration. The Madeley tithe map of 1847 shows many empty plots owned by members of the Nevett family, probably bought for speculative developments.

Dale End and the Wharfage was a scattered settlement in the eighteenth century. A few early houses are retained, but many others have been demolished or rebuilt. Of the highest status is Severn House, now the Valley Hotel, which was built around 1757 by George Goodwin, master collier and partner in the Madeley Wood Furnace Company. The house retains some of its Georgian features, and the main entrance is to the south with portico and pediment. In the 1880s it became the home of Arthur Maw, who decorated the hall and staircase with his own floor tiles and ornate majolica wall tiles.

A house east of and at right angles to the Valley Hotel, possibly a warehouse originally

58 *The Albert Edward Bridge was erected in 1864 by the Wenlock Railway Co. Of cast iron, it is a fine example of Coalbrookdale Company engineering. It is still used today, to convey coal to Ironbridge Power Station*

and with round-headed cast iron windows to the upper storey, has polychrome roof tiles in a geometric pattern by Maw & Co. This was a new line in decorative tile manufacture, but it did not take off in Britain.

Along the river bank from Dale End Park, and past the Valley Hotel, is the Albert Edward Bridge (**58**). Cast in 1863 and erected in 1864 by the Wenlock Railway Co, it was partly financed and subsequently operated by the GWR. It is still used for the transportation of coal to Ironbridge Power Station. The single-arched cast iron bridge with open spandrels containing uprights, springs from brick abutments with quoins. A plaque placed centrally reads 'Albert Edward Bridge / 1863 / John Fowler Engineer'. To the sides are further plaques: 'Cast and erected by the Coalbrookdale Company', and 'Messrs Brassey & Field, Contractors'. There is a good view of the power station from here.

Immediately east of Dale End Park is a group of long ranges, characterised by raised ridge ventilators and large round-headed openings, which now incorporate an Antiques Centre and a teddy bear factory. These made up the Severn Foundry, part of the Coalbrookdale Company, and undertaken by A. E. W. Darby in 1901. It replaced a timber yard on the site. Opposite is Yew Tree Cottage, timber-framed on a stone plinth, one of the early eighteenth-century cottages in the area. Some small stone cottages to the east are probably contemporary, while the car park opposite was the site of Nailers Row.

59 *The Coalbrookdale Company's Severn Warehouse was built in a picturesque Gothic style in the period 1838–47. The building now houses a museum of the Severn Gorge*

The most striking building on the wharfside is the former Severn Warehouse, now a visitor centre and museum (**59**). In a picturesque Gothic style with apsidal east end and decorative turrets, it was built by the Coalbrookdale Company in the period 1838–47, and may coincide with an expansion of their works when they began to concentrate on art casting. Of red and yellow brick, the detail includes crenellated parapets, moulded brickwork, buttresses, pointed arched openings and decorative iron glazing. It was clearly much more than a functional building, no doubt intended to advertise the Coalbrookdale Company. The warehouse shows that the company was still very reliant on river transport while the rest of the nation was in the grip of railway mania. It was disused by the late nineteenth century.

Some rather more functional warehouses line the Wharfage, distinguishable by their tall gable ends facing the river, with upper-storey doorways and sack hoists. Surprisingly little is known about the products that were kept there, but they are evidence of a once busy wharfside. Documentary sources suggest that they are early to mid-nineteenth century in date, but that many of them replaced earlier warehouses. Some were converted to malthouses or operated as both; the same large floor spaces and upper level doorways would have been required. There are three public houses along the Wharfage, The Swan, The Malthouse (formerly the Talbot Inn) and the White Hart. The Swan was licensed in 1805, but the Talbot Inn is earlier and retains good Georgian detail. Both these inns had malthouses, which are still standing, and they also had facilities for stabling and brewing.

60 *Bedlam is the best preserved of the generation of ironworks established in the second half of the eighteenth century. The two furnaces, one enclosed between masonry walls and under a wide brick arch, the other the brick cylindrical structure on the right, belong to rebuilding campaigns in the nineteenth century*

Beside the Malthouse pub is a bank of three lime kilns. The raw materials of limestone and coal would have been loaded into their tops while the burnt lime was drawn out from the bottom. They were constructed before 1847 and were occupied by Edward Smith, who was recorded in trade directories as being a lime-burner, maltster, and ale and porter merchant. He also owned several of the warehouses and malthouses. The lime kilns were part of the limestone quarrying operations at Lincoln Hill and there used to be further lime kilns up the hillside behind.

Further east along the Wharfage are some Victorian villas with Classical and Gothic elements. In front of no. 15 and set into the boundary wall is a cast iron milestone reading 'Shrewsbury 13 / Ironbridge 1 furlong'. A warehouse was added to the east end of the Tourist Information Centre by 1837, and is slightly reminiscent of a chapel. It has windows with shallow pointed heads, yellow brick dressings and a roundel in the gable.

Waterloo Street runs east from the centre of Ironbridge and follows the River Severn towards Coalport and Jackfield. Bedlam Furnaces, a massive monument of stone and brick, is located just outside the town (**60**). It was built by the Madeley Wood Furnace Company in 1757–9 (see **8**). On its west side are the remains of the engine house that

61 *Lloyds Engine House was a ruined, overgrown monument until its restoration. Archaeological work undertaken in conjunction with its repair revealed much new information about the former colliery pumping engine*

housed an atmospheric beam engine, with tall pump shaft behind. Water was pumped from the River Severn and was channelled into a water launder that fed a waterwheel. The wheelpit is to the east but is hidden from view. The shaft of the waterwheel powered a pair of bellows, located in the half-arched chamber, which provided the blast for one of two furnaces. However, the chamber was originally twice the width and was fronted by a complete arch. The second furnace was to the east and its bellows were driven by their own waterwheel. Raw materials were charged from the upper level — the walls of the charging houses survive but they would have been roofed originally (see **23, colour plate 2**).

By 1802–3 the bellows had been replaced by a cast iron blowing cylinder. After 1817 there were modifications to the engine and the pump shaft was enlarged. The charging houses were altered, the two furnaces were replaced and a third furnace was built further east. The new western furnace encroached upon the former bellows chamber. This furnace, encased in masonry, is visible through the wide brick fore-arch (**60**). The furnace with the tall brick stack was built later. At the same time the tuyère chamber between the two furnaces, reached by the arched passage, was rebuilt. Air was brought to the tuyère chamber in a large cast iron pipe which ran from the blowing cylinder around the back of the furnaces. From the chamber, the air was blown into the rear and sides of each furnace. The furnaces were tapped from the front, inside casting houses that no longer survive.

Paths lead up and around the charging level of Bedlam Furnaces. Further uphill is a picnic site in the location of the former brick and tile works. This was opened in 1841 following the discovery of a vein of fireclay at Styches Pit, about 1300ft (400m) to the north. It closed in 1889, after which the site was encroached upon by the Ironbridge gas works. This had been built further west, on the site of Bedlam Hall (see **8**), in 1839 and provided Ironbridge with street lighting. Some fragmentary walls survive, including a long retaining wall on the north side.

Further along the river bank towards Coalport and Blists Hill is a wall made from slag blocks, the waste product from Bedlam Furnaces. The road through Lloyds Coppice is visibly affected by geological instability. This is partly due to mining, and partly a result of natural processes. On the left-hand side is a footpath into the woods which leads to the bottom of the road which continues to Blists Hill. Near the beginning of the path is the remains of the Lloyds engine house, used for draining the local mines (see **26, 61**). The square walls of the engine house were built in 1745 and are the earliest part of the structure. Originally it housed a Newcomen-type atmospheric beam engine, but the engine was modified or replaced around 1800 and again in 1846. The power cylinder was mounted on a brick bed that defines the pit for the condensing cylinder. The brick bed is an addition, as the earliest engine would have stood on a wooden floor. The thicker south wall is the 'bob wall' on which the wooden engine beam pivoted. This beam projected outside the building and the pump rod descended into the circular brick-lined shaft. No evidence for the boilers can now be seen. A wall to the east of the engine house was the boundary of a pool, now dried up, which probably predates the engine, although its origins remain obscure.

Further into the woods, the long ridges that look like waves are a reflection of active ground movement. At the end of the path the remains of some vaulted cellars are all that is left of Madeley Wood Hall, built for the Anstice family in the early nineteenth century.

12
MADELEY

The township of Madeley contains some of the best preserved industrial monuments in the Ironbridge Gorge. Most of these have been encompassed by Blists Hill Victorian Town, which extends almost as far as Coalport, and was the initial focus of the Ironbridge Gorge Museum when it developed in the 1970s. Many of the exhibits at Blists Hill are buildings that were taken down during the development of the Telford New Town and then carefully re-erected. Although they do not form the main subject matter of this book, they provide a good cross-section of the building types of the East Shropshire Coalfield.

The majority of the structures original to the Blists Hill site are set out along the line of the Shropshire Canal, which is water-filled throughout the length of the museum. The most important structures besides the canal are the Brick & Tile Works; the Blast Furnaces; and the Hay Inclined Plane and its engine house. There were mines and adits at Blists Hill both adjacent to the canal and at a lower level. It is possible to see these remains by walking a circular route, along the canal, down part of the Hay Inclined Plane, and back through the woods at a lower level, towards the Victorian Town.

The Madeley Wood Company's Brick & Tile Works is on the east bank of the canal not far from the museum entrance (**62**). Three kilns, now ruined, stood near the canal in front of the extant drying sheds. A small, formerly barrel-vaulted drying shed stands in front of a larger (and earlier) drying shed with wide openings. There were two further drying sheds, making four in all, but these only survive below ground. The two chimney stacks were attached to the boilers, behind which the high roofs of the impressive clay preparation block can be seen. There are two clay preparation sheds with a smaller adjoining engine house. To the far left is the former office, now a museum store.

Clay was weathered for several months on the ground behind the clay preparation sheds, and was then brought onto the top floor of the western shed by a short incline. The clay-filled wagons were hauled up the rails by a horizontal steam engine made by J.C. Stevenson of Preston in 1872. This was mounted on the engine bed, a rectangular platform, inside the engine house.

The larger, eastern clay preparation shed was added between 1883 and 1902 when the arrangement of machinery inside the building must have changed. A combination of oral and archaeological evidence for this later period gives us a good idea of the processes undertaken. The weathered clay was raised up the incline as before, and was crushed between rollers before passing down through a hopper onto the middle floor, where it was stored on the platform at the back. From here it was taken into the larger shed, where there was a pan mill and mixing machines, where the prepared clay would have been extruded and cut into rough shapes. These machines are represented by brick bases and

62 *The Blists Hill Brick & Tile Works, viewed across the Shropshire Canal. The clay preparation block is between the tall boiler chimneys, with the drying sheds on the left*

63 *One of the drying sheds at the Blists Hill Brick & Tile Works. Fires were stoked at the far end and the heat was drawn into the underfloor ducts, seen here where the floor has been removed. Tile presses were located on the floor to the right*

scars on the floor. The presence of a pan mill implies that the bricks and tiles were being made by the semi-plastic process.

Power was supplied by the engine and distributed by means of line shafts and belts. The drive shafts passed through the square, cast iron bearing boxes in the walls. The engine had a limited capacity so it could only work machinery in one shed at a time, necessitating a high-level gantry allowing access to decouple the belts. Remnants of the gantry are visible in the larger shed.

When the emphasis changed to hand-made tiles and specials, the method of clay preparation varied. For example, the weathered clay could pass down through the hopper as before, but then pass directly down into a small pan mill on the ground floor, from which the clay was taken out of the front of the building into the drying sheds for hand-moulding. The drying sheds were stoked at one end, the heat passing along narrow ducts towards the flue at the other end, and then up the chimney stack (**63**). Presses were located on the floored areas. After the bricks and tiles were dried, they were fired in one of the intermittent downdraught kilns.

An early twentieth-century addition was an inclined plateway bridge across the canal, for the transportation of clay from the nearby Blists Hill Pit. The brick abutments of the bridge survive, while the deck of the bridge is lying on the ground adjacent to the working mine.

Blists Hill Pit, one of the museum's working exhibits, was sunk in the late eighteenth century (see **28**). In the mid-nineteenth century it supplied coal and ironstone to the furnaces, and latterly clay to the brick and tile works. It was abandoned in 1912. The small winding house is a reconstruction, but the winding engine itself was brought from the Milburgh Tileries in Jackfield. The wooden headgear is a replica of the original. The shaft was one of a pair; the second shaft is beneath an allotment on the opposite side of the track. Beyond it was the original winding engine house, now backfilled with earth in order to preserve it. The remains are significant because it was one of the engines built by Adam Heslop at Ketley.

Further along the canal on the right is the charging level of Blists Hill Blast Furnaces (see below). From here, the canal winds through the woods before reaching the head of the Hay Inclined Plane. Along the route are three stop locks. These are pinches with cast iron rebates into which the stop planks were lowered. One of the locks has evidence for earlier, hinged stop gates. The purpose of the stop locks was to close off sections of the canal for maintenance. It is likely that the south bank contained let-offs, through which water could be drained for this purpose.

At the end of the canal is a stone-lined basin where tub-boats would have been moored before their cargoes were loaded onto cradles to be taken down the inclined plane. There is a short counter-plane that allowed easy movement of the tubs onto the cradles. Some of the rails here are contemporary with its period of use, whilst those on the main plane have been replaced by standard-gauge rails. Opposite the apex is the remains of the engine and boiler house. A square stack stands between two circular boiler bases, which would have supported cast iron 'haystack' boilers (**64**). They were loaded with coal from the front. To the left of the boilers is a small room with stone walls, perhaps for the engine tender. The rectangular brick structure set forward on the right is the remains of the small engine house. It housed an engine by Adam Heslop, erected in early 1793. The recess beyond it, into which half an arch has collapsed, marks the position of the earliest chimney stack (more easily visible from the exterior south side). There may have been a single boiler adjacent to it. The inclined plane and its engine underwent repairs during the 1830s, but by 1847 the present boiler house and stack had been built, whilst the engine was modified, probably at the same time (**64**).

The Hay Inclined Plane worked partly by counter-balancing (see **32**). A large winding drum was erected over the apex, with a smaller, secondary winding drum to the south. The engine was used to start the movement, but the drive shaft was then disconnected as the laden boat moved downwards counter-balanced by an empty boat rising. Momentum was lost as the full boat entered the lower canal basin, so the engine was engaged again to raise the empty boat up to the sill. The engine was then attached to the secondary winding drum so that the next full boat could be raised up the counter-plane (and the empty boat lowered down it). Then the whole process would start again. When it was necessary to raise a full boat up the incline plane, far more power was required from the engine and boilers.

From the engine house, a path leads half way down the inclined plane and then turns right into the woods and towards the lower level of the blast furnaces. On the way is a reconstruction of an adit. These horizontal mines were particularly common on the

64 *One of the boiler bases for the engine at the Hay Inclined Plane. The bases supported circular 'haystack' boilers, which were stoked from the front*

south bank of the River Severn, particularly along Benthall Edge. Further along on the left are two reconstructed mines; one with wooden headgear from Ketley Bank with its brick ventilation furnace. The other is a fireclay mine from Lawley with steel headgear. Mines original to Blists Hill were also located in these woods. Close-by is St Chad's Mission Church, built of corrugated iron in 1888 to serve a mining community at Granville, north Telford.

Around this area, dotted around in the trees, are huge deposits of slag and waste dumped from the blast furnaces. Before reaching the furnaces are two reconstructed houses, a toll-house and toll gates from Thomas Telford's Holyhead Road, and a tiny stone squatter cottage, first built on common land in Little Dawley, Telford.

The best view of Blists Hill furnaces is from the lower level. The bases and hearths of the three furnaces still survive (**65**). They were tapped at the front from within three large casting houses which are now demolished (see **15, 18**). The square tapering bases would have supported the tall iron-clad furnace shafts which rose above the top of the charging houses behind. The charging houses look impressive, especially with their Gothic-style pointed arches, but they were basically retaining structures with a series of rooms immediately below charging level, which were used for maintenance activities such as black-smithing. The northernmost furnace is the earliest and with its charging house was constructed in 1832. The other two were built as a pair and were blown-in in 1840 and

1844, respectively. There are two blowing-engine houses, one to each side of the furnaces. The south engine house is dated 1840. It has considerable architectural presence with its round-headed cast iron windows, in the same tradition as non-conformist chapels. It contained a large beam blowing engine. Though removed, the interior of the engine house retains its central bob wall and deep pits. The power cylinder was located on the north side, and the blowing cylinders and flywheel on the south side. The north engine house is later (1873), but replaced the first engine house on the site, the only remnant of which is the chimney stack (**65**). A vertical blowing engine from the Lilleshall Company's Priorslee Works in Telford was inserted in 1971, similar to the original made by Stevenson of Preston. The circular hole in the front of the engine house contained a cast iron blast main that ran down into a shaft at ground-level and into a series of tunnels, from which pipes provided the air for the furnaces.

On the upper level of the furnaces, the brick walls demarcate the three charging houses. Wholesale changes occurred around 1873 when the furnace shafts were rebuilt and heightened, and the charging houses were demolished to create an open platform. A lift was used to raise the raw materials to the new level, and the circular void to the south is its associated counter-weight shaft. The raw materials were kept on iron plates before being charged, some of which still survive. To the rear of the charging area is a circular brick-lined pit with projecting iron bolts. This was the base of a calcining kiln. The steep path leading up from the lower level was an inclined plane for raising pig iron and moving coal. The rectangular brick structure at the top supported a small winding engine.

On the opposite side of the Green, set back from the Forest Glen Pavilion, is a pair of beam blowing engines known as David and Sampson. They also come from Priorslee Works and were built by Murdoch Aitken & Co of Glasgow and erected in 1851. In 1900, they were replaced by more powerful engines but were kept on standby until 1952. IGMT acquired them in 1971. They each have a power cylinder and a larger blowing cylinder that provided the blast for the furnaces. The single huge flywheel, made up of six cast iron sections, is driven by connecting rods. An element of Classical style is provided by the fluted columns that support the beam fulcrum and the valve chests. The engine in the south engine house of Blists Hill furnaces was similar to this, except that it had a single beam and cylinders.

The centre of the Victorian Town is up the hill from the Green. On the left and adjoining the railway sidings is the remains of a cast iron lattice girder bridge on brick abutments, known as Lee Dingle Bridge. It was built around 1890, replacing a timber viaduct, and carried a railway line to the Meadow Pit that supplied Blists Hill furnaces with coal.

In the twentieth century, new drying sheds and kilns were built for the Blists Hill Brick & Tile Works on the west side of the canal. One of the drying sheds, with its raised ridge vent, is now the museum's foundry. Further drying sheds stand behind the Bank and the Grocer's shop. Remains of kilns have been excavated by archaeologists beneath the foundations of the shops. One of these was known as 'The Wembley', because it was built in the same year as the stadium.

Blists Hill is part of the township of Madeley, whose origins are Saxon. The current focus is a shopping centre built in the 1960s around the Anstice Memorial Institute, a workmen's

65 *Blists Hill Blast Furnaces form one of the best preserved nineteenth-century ironworks in Britain. The blast furnace bases have survived and in the background is an engine house built in 1873. The chimney stack belongs to an earlier engine house on the site*

66 *The Anstice Memorial Institute, in the centre of Madeley, was erected in 1868 as a workmen's institute and commemorates Robert Anstice of the Madeley Wood Company*

institute erected in 1868 in memory of John Anstice of the Madeley Wood Company. It is in Italianate style with large round-headed windows to the upper storey (**66**).

The medieval focus is a small green to the south of the shopping centre. Here is the Church of St Michael, designed by Thomas Telford in 1796, which replaced the medieval church. It has an octagonal form, favoured by Telford for its auditory clarity, which though not common had precedents such as the circular Church of St Chad in Shrewsbury and the octagonal chapel at Shrewsbury Gaol, designed by John Hiram Haycock, and constructed under Telford's supervision. Telford was also aware of Methodist influence within the parish. The old church had become a centre of evangelical revival, due in large part to John Fletcher. Although the new church was built after Fletcher's death, Methodism was closely connected with the parish church for several decades afterwards, with his wife and adopted daughters taking the cause forward.

The church is constructed of large ashlar stone blocks with square windows to the lower level and tall round-headed cast iron windows above, which light the gallery. The west tower incorporates the entrance under a pediment. The short chancel with Venetian window was added later. The interior has a square three-sided gallery.

The large graveyard has memorials and gravestones to some of the key families of the area. Prominent at the entrance is the Fletcher tomb, of cast iron and painted black and white. The top slab is the memorial to John Fletcher (1729–85) and his wife Mary (1739–1815). The sides commemorate their two adopted daughters, Mary Tooth (died 1843) and Sarah Lawrence (died 1800).

On the east side of the green is the Old Vicarage, a very fine brick building of around 1700, which has five bays and three storeys with a parapet. The central shell-hood over the doorway is characteristic of this period. It was the home of John Fletcher from 1760–85. The present vicarage, a later Georgian building, is on the west side of the green. Opposite the church is the former National School dated 1841, in Tudor-Gothic style, of yellow brick with an advanced central gabled bay, and cast iron diamond glazed windows.

Further north west on Church Street is Upper House, said to have been built in 1621 by Francis Woolfe, but now much altered. The timber-framed and rendered east wing is the earliest part, with eighteenth- and nineteenth-century additions and remodelling. It was home to a number of important industrialists including John Smitheman, William Anstice and George Legge. To the west is the large barn of Upper House, a long timber-framed range with brick infill on a stone plinth. It was here that Francis Woolfe hid King Charles II on 6th September 1651 after his defeat at Worcester. Afterwards the King presented Mr Woolfe with an inscribed silver tankard, which was later sold to Richard Reynolds, finally finding its way to the Rathbone family through marriage. In the eighteenth century the barn became a Market House incorporating a shambles, whilst the three gables facing the road were probably built in the nineteenth century.

Almost opposite but mainly hidden from view is Madeley Hall, an early Georgian brick building with a five-bay east front, which was substantially extended in the 1920s and has now been converted to flats. The other end of Church Street curves round to the north east, at the end of which is a timber-framed hall-house called the Little Hay or Webb's tenement. Further north is the Fletcher Methodist Church of 1841, of yellow brick with round-headed cast iron windows and a gabled three-bay front with pilasters, a style that by now had become routine for non-conformist buildings.

Madeley Court, about half a mile north west of the town centre, was home of the Brooke family, lords of the Manor of Madeley (see **4**). They were Roman Catholics, parliamentarians and industrialists who temporarily lost their estate during the Civil War. Later, the Manor was partly owned by Abraham Darby III, and then wholly owned by Richard Reynolds. The house, now a hotel and brasserie, is L-shaped and of ashlar stone with large gabled attic dormers. The hall range, opposite the gatehouse, incorporates part of the original thirteenth-century building (a possession of Wenlock Priory) which had a wing at the south-west corner, now demolished. Flanking the hall are rooms of the fourteenth and fifteenth centuries, whilst the east wing and porch are Elizabethan, the windows with their transoms and mullions being typical of this period. Decline set in from the mid-nineteenth century after the estate was purchased by the ironmaster, James Foster. The pits sunk as part of his colliery undermined the building despite his initial wish to restore it. The house was soon unoccupied and was described in 1880 as 'fast going to decay' and 'a scene of utter desolation'. It became a farm store until 1964 when it was acquired by the Telford Development Corporation. The gatehouse, with its flanking circular turrets, is also of the late sixteenth century and was almost certainly constructed by John Brooke (**67**). It had been converted to cottages by the end of the nineteenth century. In the grounds of Madeley Court is an astronomical toy, a large square block surmounted by a hemisphere and with recesses on the sides for astronomical dials. Originally it stood on pillars 15ft (4.6m) tall.

67 *The best-preserved feature of Madeley Court is the gatehouse with its distinctive polygonal towers, erected in the late sixteenth century*

A short distance away is a restored brick building with mullioned windows, which was a water mill, connected with the priory and mentioned in Domesday. It was rebuilt as a malthouse by Basil Brooke in the early seventeenth century, when the old waterwheel was removed. It remained a malthouse until at least 1847 when it was occupied by William Dyas, a Madeley maltster, and two others. It was latterly a barn.

13
COALPORT AND JACKFIELD

Coalport and Jackfield face each other across the Severn to the east of Ironbridge. Both settlements have a strong focus on the ceramics industries and are dominated by the remains of three large factories; the Coalport Chinaworks on the north bank, and the Craven Dunnill and Maws Tileworks, both at Jackfield. There the similarities end, for Coalport was also the terminus of the Shropshire Canal where goods from the East Shropshire Coalfield were transhipped on to the River Severn. The settlement, with its industries, warehouses, wharves and workers' housing developed quickly in the late eighteenth century, but the density of buildings is now much less than it used to be. Jackfield, on the other hand, has a history going back to at least the sixteenth century and developed piecemeal. The focus changed from riverside industries, pottery and clay pipes in the seventeenth and eighteenth centuries, to bricks and tiles in the nineteenth century. Many of the houses are early, with steep narrow roofs, asymmetrical gables and tall stacks. Both sides of the river are heavily wooded, but land subsidence in Jackfield, caused by geological instability, lends a distinctive character to the area. Some paths leading down to the river were originally waggonways that took coal down to the river wharves.

Coalport runs between the Hay Inclined Plane to the west and Coalport Bridge to the east. It is dominated by the former chinaworks, now the Coalport China Museum. The brick buildings of the chinaworks are laid out between the High Street and the River Severn. The Shropshire Canal ran through the middle of the site parallel with the road but it was infilled during the 1920s (**68**). However, the west section, leading to the foot of the Hay Inclined Plane, was re-excavated in the 1970s (and restored again in the 1990s). The long building fronting the road, now a youth hostel and café, was John Rose's original china factory, started in 1795, but significantly rebuilt over the years (**68**). To the south of the former canal, workshops and kilns are set around a small courtyard which grew up from a second factory which became Reynolds (then Anstice), Horton and Rose. These two factories unified in 1814.

Most of the buildings at the China Museum are of the early 1900s, but one structure south of the canal is probably original and was certainly present by 1803. It is the remains of a biscuit kiln standing about half-height on the north-west side of the courtyard. It is quite different to the other two kilns that are about 100 years later (see **39**). Recent excavations have revealed the foundations of some other early structures, including a large range underneath the pottery workshop (adjoining the half-height kiln) and part of an enamelling kiln in front of the demonstration workshop. The western buildings running

68 *The Coalport Chinaworks, viewed from the top of one of the kilns. The Shropshire Canal, now partially restored, ran through the site. Most of the buildings belong to the early years of the twentieth century, but one of the ranges to the left of the canal is early nineteenth century. This is where John Rose's original china factory was located*

along the riverside are of about 1820, and some of the yellow brickwork is said to have come from the Caughley Chinaworks. Certainly, some of it appears to be reused or has been vitrified by intense heat.

Underneath the car park to the east of the museum are the remains of buildings for preparing the raw materials: a flint grinding mill with associated engine and boiler house, and buildings for the mixing of clay. A hitherto unknown pottery kiln was discovered along the eastern boundary of the car park during routine maintenance work in 1997, showing the potential of the site for new discoveries. Like the rest of the chinaworks much of the youth hostel dates to the early 1900s, but it is partly built off the foundations and walls of the original factory of 1795, which had a kiln at each end. However, the block that projects to the rear and houses the café is substantially unaltered and dates to the period 1803–14. There were also buildings belonging to the Coalport Chinaworks on the north side of the High Street, but there is now little to see, only a small chimney stack amongst the trees.

The Shropshire Canal was the focus of industrial enterprises at Coalport. The porcelain and pottery factories were built alongside the canal for ease of transporting raw materials and finished products. It is possible to walk along the tow-path of the reinstated section that continues to the foot of the Hay Inclined Plane. The canal basin where the tub-boats would have been moored is lined with original masonry. A second basin, now infilled, lay below the grassy bank on the north side of the canal. An impressive view of the Hay Inclined Plane can be had from the south side of the canal basin, from where the old brick road bridge is in the foreground, with a cluster of characteristic early cottages on the right (**colour plate 23**). The inclined plane is 926ft (282m) long with a vertical rise of 207ft (63m), and a gradient of 23%. It has double tracked rails relaid in the 1960s, except for those at the very bottom (and mainly underwater) which are original. Immediately south west of the canal basin is a steel footbridge leading across the River Severn to Jackfield. It is a war memorial, erected by public subscription in 1922, and replacing a former ferry service. A large memorial plaque in the centre lists the men of Coalport and Jackfield who died in the two world wars.

To the east of the canal basin is a tall house and shop, underneath which is the entrance to the tar tunnel. This was driven in 1786 by William Reynolds, to allow coal from his pits at Blists Hill to be easily conveyed to the River Severn. An underground canal was planned but never built. Instead, Reynolds hit a spring of natural bitumen. Wells were dug off the sides of the tunnel to tap more of the substance and it was brought out in horse-drawn wagons on iron plateway rails. The tunnel itself is lined in brick and built in sections, possibly to allow movement in an area of very unstable geology. Despite finding the bitumen, the tunnel did reach the Blists Hill mines and in the early days it probably was used for moving coal. The tunnel continues beyond Blists Hill towards the Madeley mines where it is of much smaller dimension and functioned as a ventilation duct. The house was built above the tunnel entrance in 1843 and bitumen production stopped around the same time.

Across the road bridge is the Shakespeare public house, the car park of which was formerly occupied by a terrace of late eighteenth-century workers' cottages known as Jug Row. A footpath leads uphill and joins the line of the former London and North Western Railway (Coalport Branch). It is now a footpath known as the Silkin Way, named after Lewis Silkin who started the New Towns movement in 1946. Immediately on the left is a bridge under the Hay Inclined Plane. It is typical of railway bridges in the Ironbridge Gorge, of blue engineering brick with a large elliptical arch on imposts. The path leads towards Blists Hill, whilst in the opposite direction the path leads to Coalport Bridge.

Immediately east of the Coalport China Museum and fronting the road is a large two-storey, seven-bay building which used to be a warehouse for storing china. It was later converted to offices. Further down the road on the right is a single storey brick building (two storeys to the rear) with a large stack and an added porch. Above the door is a sign reading 'Coalport Coffee House'. It was a literary and artistic institute by 1856 and became a temperance coffee house in 1892 with a small library and reading room. It was connected with the Coalport Chinaworks but closed down in 1917. However, this building and a smaller structure to its west had earlier origins and were part of a ropeworks in about 1800. A rope-walk would have been required to twist the rope, and the long space between the canal and the road would have been ideal. The line of the Shropshire Canal is clearly visible downstream, just behind the Brewery Inn. The pub was owned by the Coalport Chinaworks and retains early cast iron windows. Adjoining cottages were built at various times, many with original casement windows.

69 *The cast iron Coalport Bridge was erected in 1818, and replaced earlier bridges on the site. The first was a two-span wooden bridge, built in 1780. The toll-house is on the right*

Between the Brewery Inn and Coalport Bridge was the transhipment area where goods were transferred from the canal to the river, and subsequently, from railway to river. Little can now be seen of the enormous building which spanned the canal and extended out into the river (**colour plate 8**), although some masonry projecting from the riverside (and most easily seen from the south bank of the river) is part of the associated wharf. This area has high potential for future archaeological excavations. The canal ends just beyond the position of the transhipment warehouse. Coalport East station, terminus of the railway, and a large locomotive shed beyond Coalport Bridge, no longer survive.

Coalport Bridge is an attractive single-arched cast iron bridge, constructed in 1818 by John Onions, and replacing earlier bridges on the site (**69**). The first was a two-span wooden bridge of 1780, designed by William Hayward who also built a bridge over the Thames at Henley. It was rebuilt in 1791-3, and again in 1799 after it was damaged in a flood. This time it had principal half-ribs of cast iron springing from brick abutments with a timber superstructure. The present bridge is entirely of cast iron, springing from the brick abutments, and incorporating some of the earlier ironwork. The parapets are cast iron panels containing circular motifs, in the middle of which are projecting roundels bearing the name and date of the bridge. Tolls were collected at the toll-house on the north side of the bridge. It has a bay window to the front for easy visibility. Another toll-house is located at the road junction to the north, and was for those coming down the hill from Brockton. On the south side of the bridge is the former Coalport West station on the Severn Valley Railway, a yellow brick building with round-headed windows, which is now a private house.

Jackfield Bridge, further west, provides the principal road access between Coalport and Jackfield. The bridge is an elegant, modern steel design of 1994–5, which looks quite at home in its heritage context. Cable stays are attached to a single pylon at the south end which support the deck at intermediate intervals. The pylon has tubular steel legs with finials which are held together by a steel ring. This construction replaced the Free Bridge, built in 1909 by the Liverpool Hennebique Company, and an early example of reinforced concrete in bridges. A fragment of the old bridge has been kept for posterity, and is located over the south abutment. Along the narrow road towards Jackfield is a large three-bay red brick house of 1755, known as The Calcutts, in Georgian style with a central panelled door beneath a pediment.

The former Craven Dunnill Tileworks, now the Jackfield Tile Museum, is an almost perfectly preserved Victorian factory (see **44**). It consists of ranges either side of a long, narrow main yard that has gateways at both ends. The front entrance is at the west end, a passage-way through the showroom and office block, with boarded doors that have decorative, inset iron panels, and a cast iron lintel above. The windows are in Gothic style with pointed heads under which are panels of decorative tilework. The tower in the north-west corner has a spire, recently reconstructed. The showroom and office, next to the entrance, have remarkable and well-preserved internal detail (**70, colour plate 24**), while the stair hall has a mosaic floor and a tile dado.

Along the north side of the factory and facing the road (formerly the Severn Valley Railway) was a drying house, tile press shop (where tiles are again being made) and clay arks. The latter, now in a ruined state, were narrow brick bins in which the clay was allowed to weather. Behind the drying house was the kiln block — the foundations of some of the kilns still survive. On the opposite side of the main yard is a tall, steam-powered mill block for grinding the clay. A sealed up room was found inside it a few years ago, which contained a circular grinding pan and vats of red colour. Next to the mill are the blunging houses where the clay was beaten. Opposite the kiln block are the workshops where tile mosaics were made (see **43**), west of which are the former glazing shops, converted to a bronze and iron foundry in 1951. It was in this south-west corner of the site that remains of the eighteenth-century Jackfield Pottery were found, whilst the irregularly shaped walls here also appear to relate to the pottery rather than the tileworks or foundry. The factory was lit by its own purpose-built gas works, located at the south-east corner of the works. This area is bound by a wall of iron slag blocks, probably from the nearby Calcutts Ironworks.

Another notable work of Victorian architecture is Jackfield Church, located beside the Craven Dunnill Tileworks. Designed by Sir Arthur Blomfield and built in 1863, it consists of a nave, polygonal chancel, transepts and a French-style spirelet on short columns. It is constructed of banded brickwork with polychrome dressings and is said to contain bricks from all the major brick manufacturers in Jackfield. The pointed windows are in geometrical style, except for a very large rose window to the west that has a tile frieze below. The interior has tiled walls and floors, and a hand-painted tile reredos made by Maws.

70 *Decorative tiles in the former showroom of the Craven Dunnill Tileworks, now the Jackfield Tile Museum*

The old Jackfield School is opposite the main entrance of the tileworks and is dated 1844. The central entrance block has a pediment and is flanked by pilasters, beyond which are pairs of windows under square hoodmoulds. A small building behind is a brewhouse, which was attached to an earlier house on the site.

South and west of the tileworks and further uphill, are some scanty remains of the brick-making industry, now on private property but visible from the road. A stack attached to a large drying shed and a second stack belonged to the Excelsior brickworks on Chapel Road. Nearby is a cast iron beam-girder railway bridge by Brymbo of Denbighshire. Further east, the Rock brick & tile works is represented by two circular stacks on square bases. The road is named after Coalford Chapel, a small brick building now used by a local brass band.

The Severn Valley Railway passed along the north side of the Craven Dunnill Tileworks, but has now been replaced by Salthouse Road. To the east, the landscape is liable to severe landslip, and this is reflected in the very characteristic topography and the temporary road surface. The road leads to Maws, the largest of the Victorian tileworks. The former railway continues from here as the Severn Valley Way, a footpath leading to Coalport West station. To the south is a large villa on the hillside known as the Tuckies. Though constructed in the seventeenth century, and with a timber-framed west wing, the house had important connections with the industrialisation of East Shropshire. The eccentric Lord Dundonald was a tenant here from 1787. In 1800 it became the home of William Reynolds, until his death in 1803.

Less than a third of the buildings at Maws Tileworks survive, showing just how large the factory was. These surviving buildings have been converted to craft units and apartments. The entrance, as at Craven Dunnill, is at the west end and consists of a passage-way through the office block. A tiled frieze above the entrance bears the name and details of the company (**71**). The south-west corner of the block has gabled walls surmounted by a small bell tower. Inside the works is a long thin main yard with a three-storey workshop range on the right, and a two-storey workshop range on the left, all of brick, with round headed windows and saw-tooth eaves. A patch of original floor has been uncovered inside the yard, consisting of octagonal quarries and small diamond tiles with letters and geometrical motifs. Further ranges continue towards the east on the north (left) side, including a tall, four-storey mill with central hoist. Walking around the exterior of the works, the long north wall is heavily retained and buttressed due to the fall in ground level, and has a rather austere appearance. Along the south side, the gardens of the converted apartments are the site of the factory's eight main kilns, which again stood in a line.

Immediately west of Maws on the river bank is an old settlement called Salthouses. It is thought that salt was refined here in the seventeenth century or earlier. From the early eighteenth century production changed to salt-glazed stoneware, and sherds of it have been collected from the ground surface. A narrow pathway running west from the north-west corner of Maws is bounded by a wall which contains pieces of salt-glazed saggars, characterised by their shiny surface and the holes through which the salt passed to reach the stoneware which was stacked up inside.

The Jackfield Memorial Bridge, to the east of Maws Tileworks, provides easy pedestrian access to Coalport. Opposite its south end is The Boat, an eighteenth-century public

71 *The entrance to Maws Tileworks in Jackfield. The tile frieze refers to the company's history in Worcester and Benthall*

house. Terraces of workers housing run west from here, many bearing bands of decorative tiles on the front. They were built on the site of the Tuckies Brickworks before 1883, and were soon followed by the construction of Maws on the adjoining land.

14
BROSELEY AND BENTHALL

'Famous for making a great quantity of superfine tobacco pipes', Broseley was in 1746 described by Samuel Simpson as 'a very large and populous village on the Severn' but was really the urban centre of the East Shropshire Coalfield at this time. It was the south side of the River Severn in Broseley and Benthall where industry flourished first, its mineral reserves being the easiest to work, and consequently it was the first area to enter decline, despite the tobacco-pipe and brick-and-tile industries. Broseley's population actually declined in the nineteenth century and the cost of regeneration in the twentieth has been clearance for redevelopment of much that would now be regarded as heritage – mainly brickworks and slums (Broseley had 160 uninhabited houses in 1919).

The original focus of Broseley was the church, where the market was held, but the centre of the town shifted northwards to its present position in the nineteenth century. Further north is Broseley Wood, which evolved from the building of dwellings on common land in the early seventeenth century and was essentially a sprawling industrial settlement.

The church, at the south end of the town, is a good place to begin a tour of Broseley, as around it are some of its earliest and best buildings. The church was built in 1843–5 at a cost of nearly £9500, raised mainly from subscriptions. Designed by Harvey Eginton, the church is an early example of the Anglican Revival in the nineteenth century. Its Perpendicular-Gothic style, especially the tower, is derived from medieval Somerset. It is interesting to note that the new building, of dressed masonry, replaced a brick church that had been built in the early eighteenth century — masonry gave the necessary sobriety to suit contemporary ecclesiological taste.

There are several interesting houses close to the church, all of which are private residences. Perhaps the neatest is Broseley Hall, behind the church, a Georgian brick town house of five bays built c1730 for Elizabeth Crompton, owner of a large estate that included Jackfield. In the 1760s Thomas Farnolls Pritchard was commissioned to design some fireplaces and a temple for the garden. Edward Blakeway lived at Broseley Hall from the early 1770s. On the opposite side of the road is The Lawns, built in 1727 (the date is visible on a rainwater head) and purchased in 1763 by John Wilkinson. During his occupancy, the Iron Bridge was built, and before that Wilkinson employed Thomas Farnolls Pritchard to make some alterations to the building. John Rose leased the house from Wilkinson in 1800 and lived there until his bankruptcy in 1803. Although subsequently altered, principally with a large bow-fronted bay facing the road, The Lawns and Broseley Hall are similar in their use of brick with rusticated quoins at the angles, and similar to the near-contemporary Rosehill House in Coalbrookdale. The third Georgian house is Whitehall, which also retains its early character in spite of some later alteration. It was the home of John Onions in 1851. Onions owned ironstone mines, brickworks and a foundry in Broseley, and was the son of the Coneybury and Benthall ironmaster. A little further up the road is Raddle Hall, a brick house which has the date 1663 engraved on a tablet in the gable end. The house is now much altered, with enlarged windows and an added gablet.

The town centre is composed of Georgian and Victorian buildings. The centrepiece is the Victoria Hall of 1867, built for the Plymouth Brethren and with decorative tiles donated by the Maw family when it became an assembly hall about 1905. Two other buildings are worth a special mention, both on the fringes of Broseley. In King Street is the former Crown Pipeworks, now a museum and the only surviving tobacco-pipe factory building. Its entrance is now at the rear, off Duke Street, beside a former Quaker burial ground, where Abraham Darby I was buried in 1717. The Society of Friends established a meeting house here in 1691–2, and it was the sole meeting house in the coalfield until the Darby family built a new one at Coalbrookdale in 1740–1. In 1841 the Congregationalists built a new chapel next to the old meeting house, the latter being retained as a school room. The chapel was demolished in the 1960s (its site is now the car park) but part of a later school room survives as the entrance building to the Pipeworks.

Viewed from King Street, the Pipeworks gives the impression of having undergone numerous changes over time. It began as nothing more than the boundary wall of a yard, upon which buildings were constructed, probably barns and a stable originally, but which might later have been converted to a malthouse, there being numerous buildings devoted to the brewing trade in the district.

By the nineteenth century the upper floors had become a warehouse and offices, while the lower storey was divided up into small tenements. The end unit of the building was a three-storey house, its lower storey having a sash window and a panelled door, and was occupied by a local maltster. The building did not become a Pipeworks until 1881, by which time two cottages had been built in the yard behind the street. The most obvious change brought about when the Pipeworks was established by Rowland Smitheman in 1881 was the kiln in the yard (**72**).

The workshop nature of clay pipe manufacture meant that the dwellings were easy to convert, but it is unlikely that the whole block of buildings was ever devoted to pipe-making at any one time. In fact the Pipeworks had a relatively short heyday as its foundation coincided with the growing fashion for cigarettes. After Smitheman's death in 1903 his son, also Rowland, assumed control but he appears to have ceased trading about 1917. In 1923 the rival firm of William Southorn & Co bought the works, but pipe manufacture did not resume until the 1930s, and then in conjunction with slip cast pottery. By this time clay pipes had become a curiosity and their manufacture was scarcely viable as a business. The works closed in 1960 but the buildings remained unoccupied and the paraphernalia of pipe making was preserved inside them. After its purchase by Bridgnorth District Council the building has been restored. The part of the building where pipes were still made in the 1950s has been reinstated as a 'time capsule', leaving the other rooms free for exhibition space (**colour plate 25**). The Pipeworks is in fact the only surviving clay pipe manufactory in the country.

72   *The kiln at the Broseley Pipeworks was built in 1881. It was abandoned in the 1950s with pipes left inside it*

73 *Broseley Old Chapel was founded in 1741. The present building, the best preserved of the local non-conformist chapels, dates from the mid-nineteenth century. The former school room and manse is on the left*

The other building of special interest in Broseley is the Baptist chapel in Chapel Lane, on the edge of the town (**73**). The Particular Baptists built their chapel here in 1741 and by the 1770s there were over 150 members. A schism in 1801 ended when part of the congregation formed a new Baptist society and built another chapel (since demolished). A date over the entrance reads 1741 but the present building was remodelled and extended in the mid-nineteenth century and retains its cast iron window frames from that period. It has a former manse (minister's house) and school room attached. In the graveyard are buried the Broseley ironfounder John Guest (died 1788) whose son managed the Dowlais Ironworks in South Wales and provided a substantial donation to the breakaway chapel in 1801.

Benthall, like Broseley, has a riverside settlement quite distinct from the remainder of the parish. It is difficult to imagine now, crossing the Iron Bridge, how busy the south side of the river was up to half a century ago. From the bridge, the Station Hotel on the left is now the only reminder that Ironbridge station stood here, in what is now the car park. Meanwhile, on the right, was the Bower Yard Brick and Tile Works, where white bricks and firebricks were made from the late eighteenth century. Like most of the local brickworks, production ceased in the early twentieth century and sanitary pipes were subsequently made there by the Benthall Stoneware Company. The works closed in the 1950s. Although few structures have survived – the site is now a picnic area – an assortment

74 *Ironbridge Power Station is one of the most prominent landmarks in East Shropshire, dominated by its mighty cooling towers*

of sanitary pipes can be seen embedded into a bank where they act as a retaining wall to the road to Bower Yard.

Bower Yard itself was a riverside settlement where ferries plied their trade and where boats were built and maintained. The low road through the settlement passes several early houses, now mostly modernised, and ends with a bank of ruined lime kilns. A map of 1846 shows ten kilns here, most probably the result of several phases of building, although they have never been investigated in detail. Near the kilns is a railway bridge built to allow an incline tramroad to pass beneath the railway, bringing limestone from the quarries on Benthall Edge immediately above.

The landscape of quarries can be explored by following the footpaths in Benthall Edge Woods, which describe a good circular walk extending as far as Ironbridge Power Station. From the car park at the Iron Bridge, one path leads up across a bridge over the former railway and follows the line of a short incline to four collapsed adit entrances where clay was mined for the brickworks below. Higher up are more extensive limestone quarries, but still small by modern standards. The woodland is partly ancient — in the Norman period Benthall was part of the Royal Forest of Shirlett, one of seven Royal Forests in Shropshire — but is mainly secondary growth, having been re-planted after extensive felling in the nineteenth and early twentieth centuries.

75 *Benthall Hall has a fine Elizabethan front and is a late example of the style, before symmetrical fronts became fashionable*

The old Severn Valley Railway is now a public footpath. Where Benthall Edge falls steeply to the river the line continues on a viaduct by the river's edge, although it is best seen from the opposite bank of the river. The end of the surviving railway line is marked by the looming presence of one of the cooling towers of Ironbridge Power Station. Despite being tucked away at the foot of Benthall Edge, the power station dominates the landscape without detracting from it and is best viewed from a distance. The hills above Coalbrookdale and Ironbridge are good, informative vantage points (**74**), but the most dramatic is from the B4380 Ironbridge to Shrewsbury road where the power station stands above the meandering River Severn, the source of water for the steam turbines.

The first power station, Ironbridge A, opened in 1932 and was contemporary with Battersea Power Station in London. Its generators were shut down finally in 1978 and the station was demolished in 1982–3. The present Ironbridge B power station was built in the 1960s in the wake of the exponential growth of electricity consumption in the post war years, and was linked to the national grid in 1969. A fine example of modernist architecture, the white cubic masses of its switch house contrast with the reddish-brown curving forms of its four cooling towers, a bold composition for the head of the Severn Gorge.

The original village of Benthall was built around the parish church but has subsequently shrunk away, leaving the church looking like an adjunct of the adjacent Benthall Hall. The church is an old foundation, as early as 1221, but the present church of St Bartholemew was built in 1667, a likeable but not especially distinguished building. Its large sundial, above a sculpted lion's head, was added in 1893 over the original south door. In the churchyard are some interesting cast iron grave slabs including one dedicated to Eustace Beard, one of the family of local trowmen, who died in 1761.

Benthall Hall, which stands behind the church, is one of the most important Elizabethan country houses in Shropshire (**75**). It probably occupies the site of an earlier manor house, but the present house was built by Lawrence Benthall in about 1580. Its main front, facing across a lawn to the church, is notable for its asymmetrical composition, consisting of groups of star-shaped brick chimneys, gabled bays and two polygonal bay windows flanking a square porch, itself offset from the centre. The façade is one of the last examples of medieval planning based on a great hall, which accounts for the asymmetry, before Renaissance ideas prescribed symmetrical fronts with internal planning to match, and classical details. The porch carries five stone tablets, known as a quincunx, which are thought to represent the stigmata, a sign that the owners were Roman Catholics.

Inside is a richly carved Jacobean staircase, dated 1618. The plaster detail in the west drawing room is similarly lavish and was added in about 1630. The building was attacked in 1645 during the Civil War and in 1818 was damaged by fire. In the subsequent rebuilding a new wing was added. In the eighteenth and nineteenth centuries it was home to local entrepreneurs such as the potter John Thursfield and George Maw. The Benthall family did not buy it back until 1934. The family still live there but in 1958 it was handed to the care of The National Trust.

GLOSSARY

Cast iron   Iron with a carbon content of 3-4%. It is not malleable, but can be melted and poured into moulds and is strong in compression, making it suitable for many engineering purposes.

Earthenware   Vessels made of clay with inclusions such as flint. There was a wide variety of earthenwares, from domestic coarse wares to refined creamwares and pearlwares, some of which resembled porcelain.

Kiln   An oven for firing pottery, bricks, tiles or clay pipes. Kilns were constructed with fireboxes around a circular or rectangular chamber where the items were fired. In a downdraught kiln the heat rose to the top of the kiln and was then drawn down through the kiln chamber and along a flue to a detached chimney. Downdraught kilns produced a more even heat than updraught kilns, where the heat passed up through the kiln chamber from the fireboxes below to a chimney on the top. In the brick and tile industry, 'intermittent kilns' had a single chamber which was allowed to cool after firing, but they were less efficient than 'continuous kilns' which had several chambers and where the heat was maintained.

Pan mill   A large circular pan with a perforated base. Clay was ground to a powder by large iron 'runners', much like solid wheels, and passed down through the bottom.

Pig iron   Iron cast direct from a blast furnace into long bars formed by sand moulds. Pig iron is a crude form of cast iron and was re-melted for casting or further refined to make wrought iron.

Plateway   A simple track laid with iron plates that are L- shaped in cross section, also known as a tramway. Plateways were commonly used in the nineteenth century for horse-drawn wagons, replacing the earlier wooden railways or 'waggonways'. Plateways should not be confused with railways, where flanged wheels run on top of edge rails.

Porcelain   A translucent ceramic material made from special clays and other ingredients, such as ground flint or bone. The purpose was to imitate Chinese pottery. 'Soft' porcelain was introduced into Britain in the 1760s. The first 'hard' paste European porcelain was made at Meissen, Germany, in 1709 and was made in the Potteries, Derby and Worcester by the 1780s.

Pug mill   In brick and tile making, a machine used for mixing clay or other material with a little water, usually consisting of a central shaft to which blades are fitted. Pugging produces even-textured clay and adds to the strength of the fired product. A bat machine is a variation of a pug mill used in tile making, where clay was extruded in a continuous strip and cut into bats on a table with wire cutters. Bats were slightly larger than finished tiles.

Saggar   In the pottery industry, a round, flat-bottomed ceramic bowl used to protect wares during firing and to ensure even heating.

Steel   An alloy of iron containing up to 1.5% carbon. It can be hammered and rolled like wrought iron. Steel gave harder edges to wrought iron. Modern steel is much like wrought iron but cheaper to produce.

Stoneware   Vessels made from clay and sand fired at a very high temperature, so that the minerals fuse.

Wrought iron   In practical terms, pure iron, containing only small quantities of other elements, in particular about 0.05% carbon. When heated it can be hammered or rolled into various shapes, or welded.

FURTHER READING

Ironbridge has generated no shortage of literature and the nature of the subject makes it readily accessible to the non-specialist. The list below gives the most relevant published works. The library of the Ironbridge Gorge Museum Trust, open by appointment, has a comprehensive collection of literature and documentary sources relating to the area.

General works

Alfrey, J., and Clark, C., 1993, *The Landscape of Industry: Patterns of Change in the Ironbridge Gorge*. London: Routledge

Baugh, G.C. (ed), 1985, *The Victoria History of the Counties of England: A History of Shropshire*, Vol XI. London: University of London Institute of Historical Research

Crossley, David, 1990, *Post-Medieval Archaeology in Britain*. Leicester: Leicester University Press

Hayman, R., Horton, W. and White, S., 1999, *Archaeology and Conservation in Ironbridge*. York: CBA

Pevsner, Nikolaus, 1958, *The Buildings of England: Shropshire*. Harmondsworth: Penguin

Randall, John, 1879, *History of Broseley*. Madeley: the author

Randall, John, 1880, *History of Madeley, including Ironbridge, Coalbrookdale and Coalport*. Madeley: the author

Stratton, Michael, 1994, *Ironbridge and the Electric Revolution*. London: John Murray

Trinder, Barrie, 1982, *The Making of the Industrial Landscape*. London: Dent

Trinder, Barrie, 1996, *The Industrial Archaeology of Shropshire*. Chichester: Phillimore

Trinder, Barrie, 2000, *The Industrial Revolution in Shropshire*, 3rd edition. Chichester: Phillimore

Trinder, B., and Cossons, N., 2002, *The Iron Bridge*. Chichester: Phillimore

Contemporary sources

Birch, Alan, 1952, 'Midlands Iron Industry during the Napoleonic Wars', *Edgar Allen News* 31, 231-3

Chaloner, W.H., 1949, 'Smelting Iron Ore with Coke and Casting Naval Cannon in the Year 1775: Marchant de la Houlière's Report on English Methods, Part 2', *Edgar Allen News* 27, 213-15

Flinn, M.W. (ed), 1973, *Svedenstierna's Tour of Great Britain 1802–3: The Travel Diary of an Industrial Spy*. Newton Abbot: David & Charles

Morgan, Kenneth (ed), 1992, *An American Quaker in the British Isles: the travel journals of Jabez Maud Fisher, 1775–1779*. Oxford: Oxford University Press

Plymley, Joseph, 1803, *General View of the Agriculture of Shropshire*. London: McMillan

Scarfe, Norman (ed), 1995, *Innocent Espionage: The La Rochefoucauld Brothers' Tour of England in 1785*. Woodbridge: Boydell Press

Trinder, Barrie (ed), 1979, *Coalbrookdale 1801: a contemporary description*. Ironbridge: IGMT

Trinder, Barrie (ed), 2005, *'The Most Extraordinary District in the World': Ironbridge and Coalbrookdale*, 3rd edition. Chichester: Phillimore

Iron, coal and related industries

Cox, Nancy, 1990, 'Imagination and Innovation of an Industrial Pioneer: the First Abraham Darby', *Industrial Archaeology Review* 12/2, 127-44

Griffiths, Samuel, 1873, *Griffiths' Guide to the Iron Trade*. London: the author (facsimile edition 1967, David & Charles, Newton Abbot)

Hayman, Richard, 1997, 'Lloyds Engine House, Ironbridge', *Transactions of the Shropshire Archaeological and Historical Society* 72, 38-51

Hyde, Charles, 1977, *Technological Change in the British Iron Industry, 1700–1870*. Princeton: Princeton University Press

Jones, N.W., 1987, 'A Wooden Waggonway at Bedlam Furnace, Ironbridge', *Post-Medieval Archaeology* 21, 259-62

Lewis, M.J.T., 1970, *Early Wooden Railways*. London: Routledge and Kegan Paul

Mott, R.A., 1958, 'The Shropshire Iron Industry', *Transactions of the Shropshire Archaeological Society* 56, 68-81

Mott, R.A., 1961, 'The Coalbrookdale Group Horsehay Works: Part I', *Transactions of the Newcomen Society* 31 (for 1957–9), 43-56

Mott, R.A., 1961, 'The Coalbrookdale Group Horsehay Works: Part II', *Transactions of the Newcomen Society* 32 (for 1959–60), 271-88

Mott, R.A., 1983, *Henry Cort: The great Finer*. London: The Metals Society

Raistrick, Arthur, 1989, *Dynasty of Ironfounders*, 2nd edition. Ironbridge: IGMT

Thomas, Emyr, 1999, *Coalbrookdale and the Darbys,* York: Sessions Book Trust

Wanklyn, M.D.G., 1973, 'Iron and Steelworks in Coalbrookdale 1645', *Shropshire Newsletter* 44, 3-6

Wanklyn, M.D.G, 1982, 'Industrial Development in the Ironbridge Gorge before Abraham Darby', *West Midlands Studies* 15, 3-7

Pottery and china

Barker, D., and Horton, W., 1999, 'The development of the Coalport Chinaworks', *Post-Medieval Archaeology* 33, 3-93

Barrett, F.A., 1951, *Caughley and Coalport Porcelain*. Leigh-on-Sea

Edmundson, R.S., 1981, 'Bradley & Co, Coalport Pottery, 1796–1800', *Northern Ceramic Society Journal* 4, 127-55

Godden, G.A., 1981, *Coalport and Coalbrookdale Pottery*, 2nd edition. London: Herbert Jenkins

Jewitt, Llewellynn, 1878, *The Ceramic Art of Great Britain*. London: Virtue & Co

Messenger, Michael, 1995, *Coalport 1795–1926*. Woodbridge: Antique Collectors' Club

Bricks, tiles and pipes

Furnival, William, 1904, *Leadless Decorative Tiles, Faience and Mosaic*. Stone: the author Hayman, R. and Horton, W., 1999, 'Broseley Pipeworks', *Industrial Archaeology Review* 21/1, 25-39

Herbert, Tony and Huggins, Kathryn, 1995, *The Decorative Tile in Architecture and Interiors*. London: Phaidon Press

Kay, Geoffrey, 1992, 'Charles Lynam - An Architect of Tile Factories', *Journal of the Tiles and Architectural Ceramics Society* 4, 21-8

Strachan, Shirley, 1990, 'Henry Powell Dunnill: A Victorian Tilemaster', *Journal of the Tiles and Architectural Ceramics Society* 3, 3-9

Walker, I.C., 1976, 'Churchwarden Clay Tobacco-Pipes and the Southorn Pipemaking Family of Broseley, Shropshire', *Post-Medieval Archaeology* 10, 142-9

Social and cultural history

Daniels, Stephen, 1992, 'De Loutherbourg's Chemical Theatre: Coalbrookdale by Night', in John Barrell (ed), *Painting and the Politics of Culture: New Essays on British Art, 1700–1850*, 195-230. Oxford: Oxford University Press

Friedman, Terry, 1996, 'The Golden Age of Church Architecture in Shropshire', *Transactions of the Shropshire Archaeological and Historical Society* 71, 83-134

Gattrell, V.A.C., 1994, *The Hanging Tree: Execution and the English People 1770–1868*. Oxford: Oxford University Press

Ionides, Julia, 1998, *Thomas Farnolls Pritchard of Shrewsbury: Architect and Inventor of Iron Bridges*. Ludlow: Dog Rose Press

Klingender, Francis, 1972, *Art and the Industrial Revolution*, 2nd edition. London: Granada

Muter, W. Grant, 1979, *The Buildings of an Industrial Community: Coalbrookdale and Ironbridge*. Chichester: Phillimore

RCHME, 1986, *An Inventory of Nonconformist Chapels and Meeting Houses in Central England*. London: HMSO

Skinner, R.F., 1964, *Nonconformity in Shropshire, 1662–1816*. Shrewsbury: Wilding & Son

Smith, Stuart, 1979, *A View from the Iron Bridge*. Ironbridge: IGMT

Index